The Plays of
AESCHYLUS

ROBERT H. AHRENS, JR.
ASSISTANT PROFESSOR OF ENGLISH
SETON HALL UNIVERSITY

"Independent Writers"
P.O. Box 104
Woods Hole, MA 02543

MONARCH
PRESS

Published by
MONARCH PRESS
a Simon & Schuster division of
Gulf & Western Corporation
Simon & Schuster Building
1230 Avenue of the Americas
New York, N.Y. 10020

MONARCH PRESS and colophon are trademarks
of Simon & Schuster, registered in the U.S. Patent
and Trademark Office.

Standard Book Number: 0-671-00801-3

Library of Congress Catalog Card Number: 66-27253

Printed in the United States of America

CONTENTS

LIFE, STYLE, AND THEMES OF AESCHYLUS

LIFE: Though there are few facts known concerning Aeschylus' life, the following may be stated with some assurance. He was born at Eleusis, a city northwest of Athens, in 525 B.C. His father, Euphorion, belonged to the old Athenian nobility, the "Eupatridae." Aeschylus is said to have presented his first dramas in 499, at the age of twenty-six. In 490 he participated in the battle of Marathon, in which his brother Cynaegirus was killed. He won his first dramatic victory in 484, with a play no longer extant. In 481 the Persians won the battle of Thermopylae, and Aeschylus and the rest of the Athenian population left the city. He returned with his fellow-citizens in 480 after he had taken part in the brilliant Athenian naval victory at Salamis. He made a number of visits to Syracuse, in Sicily, during and after the lifetime of Hiero the First, tyrant of Syracuse, who ruled from 478-467, and for whom Aeschylus exhibited a number of his plays.

Aeschylus died in 456 B.C. in Gela, in Sicily, where he was also buried. On his tomb was placed this epitaph: "Beneath this stone lies Aeschylus, son of Euphorion, the Athenian, who perished in the wheat-bearing land of Gela; of his noble prowess the grove of Marathon can speak, or the long-haired Persian who knows it well." Who wrote this epitaph is not known, but many people feel that only Aeschylus himself could have praised the soldier and remained silent about the poet. He had, after all, exhibited between eighty and ninety dramas during his lifetime, and had won the prize at least thirteen times. He was the most commanding figure among the tragedians of 500-458, and for more than half that time he was usually the victor in the contests. Unfortunately, of Aeschylus' plays only seven are extant.

STYLE: No one contributed more to the development of Greek

5

tragedy than Aeschylus. When he was young the drama was primarily choral, with some rudimentary action between the chorus and a single masked actor added. When he began to write plays himself, he therefore had to choose between this near-ritual and what we would call "theatre," between chorus and drama. He himself was a professional director of choruses, and could be expected to be partial to the sung and danced portions. Indeed, his choruses are the longest in Greek drama; even in the *Agamemnon*, his most fully developed tragedy, there are only 900 lines of dialogue out of a total of about 1,670 lines. Nonetheless, Aeschylus did enlarge significantly the acted portions of his plays, and in a further attempt to overcome the static quality of the established form of drama he took a great step by adding a second tragic actor. Later, after Sophocles had introduced yet a third actor, Aeschylus made use of this innovation as well.

DECLINE OF THE CHORUS: By increasing the number of actors and the number of lines given over to them, the importance of the chorus and the number of lines assigned to it necessarily had to be decreased. As a result, Aeschylus was able to reduce the size of the chorus from a relatively unwieldy fifty to a compact twelve to fifteen. Thus, while the chorus was less important than it had been, Aeschylus was enabled to integrate it much more dramatically with the actors. This, in turn, made it possible for him to delve much more deeply into the inner being of each of the characters he portrayed. So by adding a second actor, who could impersonate several characters, by extending the action of the play, deepening characterization, and intensifying the dramatic function of the chorus, Aeschylus became the world's first great dramatist. He is, indeed, known as "the father of tragedy."

PLOTS AND CHARACTERIZATION: While presenting a good deal of variety through the use of his innovations, it is interesting that Aeschylus' plots remained quite simple and the action in his plays relatively static. He is occasionally vague as to time and setting, the entrances and exits of his characters are often awkward, and the characters themselves undergo little or no development. Yet his characters possess a stark and majestic grandeur, his tragedies have an epic quality, and his language is exalted, though sometimes bombastic. In addition, it was Aeschylus who originated the trilogy on one unified theme. This made it possible for him to explore in depth the themes he presented, to be a dramatist of ideas who could often employ symbolism.

OTHER INNOVATIONS: Surprisingly, perhaps, Aeschylus was something of a sensationalist. Many of his characters are weird impersonations of natural forces and fantastic mythological figures. In the *Eumenides,* for example, he brought the Furies on the scene so realistically that he was reputed to have frightened children and to have caused women in the audience to have miscarriages. At least part of this effect was the result of the costumes worn by the Furies, costumes which had been designed by Aeschylus himself. In fact, Greek tradition credits him with the invention of tragic costume, but this is probably incorrect. He does seem, however, to have been responsible for the invention of the tragic boot called the *cothurnus,* which was intended to give added stature to the actors, and which is described later. Aeschylus was also the first to decorate the front of the *skene* with screens and other props required by his specific play, and apparently he was the first to employ machinery and scenic effects successfully. Consequently, he was the theatre's first notable showman, as well as its first important playwright, stage director, costumer, and dancing master. Before his death, therefore, he enjoyed the dual satisfaction of seeing a theatre replete with action, movement, and color, and knowing that it was largely his own creation.

THEMES: Aeschylus' mind was constantly concerned with ethical problems, with questions of guilt, hereditary evil, and divine justice, and here he was an innovator, too. He virtually dismissed the polytheism of his time and closely approached monotheism. He regarded Zeus as the guardian of justice and as a god far removed from the willful and rather immoral divinities who appear in the Homeric poems. In addition, he conceived of God as a developing personality or principle which grows in goodness with the passage of time. He also makes it clear in his plays that he saw an evolutionary principle in nature, for he asserts that Fate or Necessity, which orders everything, ensures the development of divine law in the direction of greater altruism and justice. In the realm of human behavior, Aeschylus mediates between the primitive blood feud and civilized order. In the *Oresteia,* his last trilogy, he arrives at the conclusion that it is the evil in man and not the envy of the gods that destroys happiness. His main themes, therefore, present the triumph of justice over violence, personal responsibility and the possibility of retribution for sin, the punishment of pride, self-will, and sacrilege, the inherent limitations of man, and the concept that life is basically tragic but that wisdom emerges from suffering.

EXTANT PLAYS: *The Suppliant Maidens,* traditionally dated c. 490 B.C., which if correct would make this the earliest surviving drama. A recently published papyrus indicates, however, that the trilogy of which this play is a part might not have been first produced until after 470 B.C.

The Persians, 472 B.C. If the papyrus mentioned above is correct, then this is the earliest produced surviving drama.
Seven Against Thebes, 467 B.C.
Prometheus Bound, date unknown.
Agamemnon, 458 B.C.
The Libation Bearers, 458 B.C.
The Eumenides, 458 B.C.
The last three plays, *Agamemnon, The Libation Bearers,* and *The Eumenides,* make up the *Oresteia,* the only surviving trilogy by Aeschylus.

KNOWN LOST PLAYS: *Alcmena; Amymone; The Argives; The Argo; Atalanta; Athamas; The Bacchae; The Cabiri; Callisto; Cercyon; The Chantriae; The Children of Heracles; Circe; The Daughters of Danaus; The Daughters of Phorcys; The Daughters of the Sun; The Dictyolloi; The Edonians; The Egyptians; The Epigonoi; Europa; The Female Archers; Glaucus; Glaucus of the Sea; Glaucus of Potniae; The Heralds; Hypsipyle; Iphigenia; Ixion; The Judgment of the Armor; Laius; The Lemnians; Lion; Lycurgus; Memnon; The Men of Eleusis; The Myrmidons; The Mysians; The Necromancers; Nemea; The Nereids; The Net-Drawers; Niobe; The Nurses of Dionysus; Oedipus; The Ostologoi; Oreithyia; Palamedes; Pentheus; The Perrhaebians; Penelope; Perseus; Phineus; Philoctetes; The Phrygians; Polydectes; The Priestesses; Prometheus the Fire-Bringer; Prometheus Unbound; The Propomp-*

*poi; Proteus; The Ransom of Hector; The Salaminiae; Sem-
ele; Sisyphus; The Sphinx; Telephus; The Thracian Women;
The Theoroi; The Women of Aetna; The Women of Crete;
The Women of the Fawn-Skin; The Weighing of Souls; The
Youth.*

THE DEVELOPMENT OF
FIFTH CENTURY ATHENS

ORIGIN OF THE GREEKS: It is difficult to trace the origin of the Greeks with any real certainty. Scholars agree that the historical Greeks were most likely the result of a slow fusing of Achaean and other invaders from the north and the people they found already living in the Aegean world. The descendants of these early Greeks then migrated to the islands and Asiatic shores of the Aegean Sea, sometimes coming into conflict with the descendants of other groups of the earlier invaders. It is quite possible that the memory of one or more of these conflicts is embodied in the story of the Trojan war, the traditional date of which is 1184 B.C. The date, and even the war itself, might be traditional, but the city was a fact. Heinrich Schliemann, the German archaeologist, excavated the site of Troy during the years 1871 to 1875. These migrations of the Greeks across the Aegean took place between 1300 and 1000 B.C.

While these events were taking place the Dorians, the ancestors of the Spartans, spilled into Central and Western Greece and gradually moved south, finally occupying most of the Peloponnesus, Crete, Rhodes, and parts of Asia Minor. By the time these migrations ended, about 900 B.C., the Greeks and their language and customs were well established on both sides of the Aegean Sea.

THE GREEK CITY-STATES: Although the early history of the Greeks is obscure, the development of the city-states must have begun early, for by the eighth century B.C., the earliest time for which records exist, the city-states were well established, and in the more advanced communities laws and constitutions were beginning to appear. It is important to remember that Greece was not a single, large state. Race and language constituted the national bond, not politics. Competition between the hundreds of city-states ranged from athletics to religion. Although all Hellenes were devoted to athletics, each city desired supremacy in one or another sport, and while all Greeks held to the same basic religion, there were innumerable local variations. Thus, though the art, poetry, and science that developed in different cultural centers rapidly became a common possession of all, the Greeks did not feel the need of political unity as an aid to civilization.

THE POLIS: The *polis*, or city-state, was responsible for the development of almost all of the outstanding Greek characteristics. Its small size enabled all citizens to realize and experience the problems, moral and economic, which confront men in all ages and communities as they try to develop the basic conditions of a worthy civic life. In the city-states the Greeks achieved the union of civilized life and political liberty, and they were the first to do so. In Homer, the polis was first and foremost a defensible fortress. This attitude explains why the Acropolis was built on a rocky hill, and, for that matter, why most Greek temples were built on elevated ground at the heart of the city.

In time the individual Greek family became less important than the community family, and the polis was at all times visible to the naked eye of every citizen whether he was farming in the outskirts or conversing within the city's walls. Everyone in the community knew everyone else by sight and each, rich or poor, ruler or ruled, had a personal relationship to the others. Since the Greeks were an agricultural people who cultivated corn, grapes, and olives, they lived a good part of their lives outdoors and they had substantial stretches of leisure. This leisure was spent in social intercourse and the gaining and display of intellect and talent. The only life truly worth living was that of citizen service, and the Greek word for virtue (*aretê*) expressed not only moral excellence but also intellectual talent and the capacity to succeed in every field of public life.

SOCIAL LIFE AND THE POLIS: In the Greek scheme of things it was the male who was all-important. His mother, and later his wife, had no soul and therefore did not count. In both their daily lives and their formal assemblies Greek men had freedom of thought and speech, and they talked chiefly about what was most worthy of being discussed: law and freedom, moral duty and the purpose of government, the nature and causes of things, art and poetry, virtue and the well-being of man. Moreover, their talk was reasoned and logical, the expression of clear thinking and grasp of fact, and they translated their thought into the communal and political action of the polis. One natural result of their logic was that while the free population of a city included men, women, and children, only the men could vote. Another was that there was no distinction between church and state: the magistrate presided over the religion of the city, while the priesthood discharged the ceremonial duties.

WRITERS AND THE POLIS: The dramatists and historians of the fifth century constantly wrote of their sense of the value of the polis as the provider of scope for the realization of the good life. The philosophers taught that the only life worth living was that of the citizen in the Hellenic city-state. Socrates, after being condemned by the Athenians, was offered the chance to escape and turned it down, asserting that to evade the law of the polis, even though unjustly exercised, was morally wrong. Plato condemned all of the existing Greek city-states as corrupt beyond saving, yet he outlined in his *Republic* an ideal community that was really a reformed Hellenic polis. Aristotle later defined the polis, in his *Politics*, as "an association formed for the maintenance of complete and self-sufficient life; other forms of association enable man to live, but the polis alone enables him to live well," and he defined man as a "political animal." The main functions of the lawgiver, therefore, were the development of moral goodness in the citizen, and his education to the complete achievement of the capacities of his nature in the city-state.

SEEDS OF DESTRUCTION WITHIN THE POLIS: But while the polis contained all of these things, it contained another factor as well, something inherently destructive which eventually brought about the downfall and conquest of the Greek city-states. Freedom is sometimes a dangerous thing, and complete freedom can be the most completely dangerous of all. The life of the polis gave freedom alike to civic patriotism and personal ambition. Civil discord, *stasis*, was the chronic disease of the polis. It showed itself in two forms: the inability of states to combine in a viable political union even in the face of a common foe, and the internal strife caused by men, families, and parties within a single community. There were many shifting confederations of cities formed to fight common foes, but these were transient, and when Macedon and Rome marched, the confederations were unavailing. And it was Plato who traced the source of public tyranny in the state to the tyranny of lawless passion within the individual. He saw that it was the most gifted of the citizens who were most tempted to become victims of the lust for power, and who then shattered first the harmony of their own souls and then that of the polis.

For all its splendid achievements, Greek history is full of tragedy, its pages strewn with the wreckage of ruined lives. They represent the noblest sacrifice it is possible to make: the sacrifice by which the mind of man purchases its freedom to think and act. It is no wonder that the Greek theatre was chiefly a forum for tragedy.

DEVELOPMENT OF TYRANNY: The eighth and seventh centuries were largely marked by commercial development, the growth of wealth and social refinement, political unrest, colonization, and the rapid spread of the city-state over the islands and coasts of the Mediterranean. As a result of the growth of commerce, a class of merchant princes developed, and as this new plutocracy contested with the old nobility for power and privilege the political arena seethed with ferment and revolution. The rivalry between men of birth and wealth, and of land and trade, caused a vacillation between democracy and despotism, and led to the rise of that form of government known to the Greeks as "tyranny."

It often happened that a rich merchant, after obtaining popular support, would overthrow an oppressive oligarchy of nobles and establish himself as a despot. Surprisingly, the "tyrants" were often enlightened and humane rulers, but they offended the intense Greek love of freedom; consequently, their rule usually created bitter resentment. Because they set themselves above the law, by their means of obtaining power and exercising it, they thereby forfeited any claim to its protection. Moreover, the

Greeks had an intense antipathy toward power based on possession of wealth. Theognis of Megara summed up the Greek attitude when he wrote, "To lay low a tyrant who consumes the people is no sin and will not be punished by the gods." The development of law and political institutions during these centuries was greatly aided by the advances toward democracy which resulted from the breaking down of hereditary privilege. Of equal, or perhaps even greater importance, was the parallel expansion of culture in the areas of poetic literature, art, philosophy, and science. Of these, the most important from the point of view of Greek drama is poetic literature.

DEVELOPMENT OF POETIC LITERATURE: The earliest Greek poems which we possess are the two epics ascribed to Homer, the *Iliad* and the *Odyssey*, which were composed some time between 1200 and 800 B.C. (Homer himself is usually dated between 900 and 800 B.C.). The world portrayed in these two poems is a real world of which two features stand out most prominently. First, the life depicted is that of a feudal aristocracy. One is told little of the common people, and they play no part in the action. Indeed, the slaves themselves are captives of princely birth. But this poetry was not popular poetry meant for the enjoyment of the common people. It was composed by minstrels for noble chieftains, and sung to the honor of their families and clans. Second, despite this inherently undemocratic character, there is nonetheless an air of freedom in the Homeric world. There is no political despotism, no priestcraft; both intrigue and magic are rare; women live on a high level of equality with men and enjoy great respect in the household; and slaves and their masters speak to each other on almost equal terms as men to men.

LYRIC AND ELEGIAC POETRY: The early epics, of which the *Iliad* and the *Odyssey* are the only two surviving examples, told tales of famous men and heroic action. Later poets were more subjective and more romantic, and it was the epoch of commercial expansion that saw the birth of lyric and elegiac poetry. This poetry was richly varied in subject and metrical form, and included poems of love and war, sorrow and boredom (ennui), as well as the dirge and the marriage-song, choric odes, and political and personal satire. In addition, the growing interest in moral reflection gave rise to didactic poetry which expressed criticism of life, counsels of policy or prudence, and precepts of public and private action. This type of poetry is of special significance when one remembers that in the Greek view it was the poets rather than the priests who were the recognized teachers of moral and religious truth.

ROLE OF THE POETS: It was part of the function of the poets to narrate and interpret the tales of gods and heroes, and they were allowed great latitude in the selection and reconstruction of their material. First the didactic poets, and then Pindar and the fifth-century dramatists, attempted to adjust poetic teaching to the growing moral consciousness of the time. It was during this epoch that proverbial maxims such as "know thyself," "nothing in excess," and "rule will reveal the man," all of which represented popular inductions from moral experience, became immensely popular and meaningful to the Greeks, and the conception of an ethical standard took shape in the ideal of *sôphrosynê*.

SOPHROSYNE: The essential meaning of sôphrosynê was self-restraint and obedience to law, whether the law of the state or of the inner principle of self, especially in the face of any temptation to abuse wealth and power or to subordinate civic loyalty to personal ambition. Additionally it implied a clear vision, the result of self-knowledge, which would enable a person or a community to act with a balanced judgment at any critical moment. Summed up in one word: moderation.

HUBRIS: The opposite of this saving wisdom was *hubris*: the violent overstepping of the mark, the insolence of wealth or triumph, the pride of life and self that trampled underfoot the unwritten law of gods and men. Hubris was the nearest Greek equivalent for "sin." It was most typically found in the insatiable thirst for power which drove man or state headlong on the path of self-assertion and domination. This overriding passion, which violated both personal liberty and public law, lured the victim, by way of a frenzy of self-confidence, toward destruction, and it provoked *nemesis*, the feeling of righteous indignation, in the gods and in his fellow men. When tyranny appeared, it was regarded as the crowning manifestation of hubris in the public life of the city-state. In addition, as Aeschylus said in *Agamemnon*, "An ancient hubris ever breeds a fresh and living hubris to add to human woes." Consequently, Greek poets, attempting to give the proper due to both inherited fatality and individual desert, depicted the gathering cloud of doom that visited the sins of the fathers on the children through successive generations of a sinful race.

FIFTH-CENTURY ATHENS: Athens in the fifth century was the leading commercial and political city of the Greek world, and it was there that Greek civilization reached its greatest heights. All the currents of literature, art, and knowledge met and flowed there to produce a wealth and variety of creative genius such as never before or after appeared in one place at one time. In this one city-state, whose free population was about 250,000 (a figure which includes men, women, and children, but not slaves or resident aliens), there lived within the span of three human generations such statesmen as Themistocles and Pericles; the tragic poets Aeschylus, Sophocles, and Euripides, and the comic poet Aristophanes; the sculptor Phidias and his school; the historians Herodotus and Thucydides; and the philosophers and teachers Anaxagoras, Socrates, and Plato. There were many, many others who were overshadowed by these, but who themselves would be ranked among the most famous men of history had they lived in any other age.

GROWTH AND REFORMS: Athens had originally had an economic system based upon agriculture, but her proximity to the sea and her harbor of Piraeus enabled her to enter wholeheartedly into the expansion of trade, with the result that she developed into a great commercial city. Because during her agricultural days political privileges had been restricted to landowners, the transition to commerce created unrest. Solon, an aristocrat with moderate political views, sole *archon*, or magistrate, was, in 594 B.C., the first to allow merchants to qualify for active citizenship and public office. He also reformed the criminal law, and, more importantly, instituted the Popular Assembly (*Ecclesia*) to which the magistrates were accountable. This latter reform laid the first true foundation of popular democracy.

The tyranny of Pisistratus and his sons, Hipparchus and Hippias (560-510 B.C.), was remarkable for its respect for law and constitutional procedure, its encouragement of agriculture and trade, and its great stimulus to art and culture. Ironically, the thirst for political equality, once stimulated, was uncompromising and unquenchable: Hipparchus was murdered and a revolution forced Hippias to flee the city. In 508 B.C. reforms brought about by Cleisthenes resulted in the first truly democratic government in the history of the world. He admitted alien residents to full citizenship and made all citizens politically equal. All magistrates and the board of generals were elected by all citizens, and the Ecclesia, in which all citizens had the right to vote, became the supreme lawmaking body.

PERSIAN WARS: The Persians had already subjugated the Asiatic Greeks, and their navy threatened to convert the Aegean into a Persian sea. The Ionian Greeks, with the support of Athens, revolted early in the fifth century, but the revolt was crushed by the Persians in 494 B.C. In 490 a punitive expedition led by Darius was sent by sea against the Athenians, whose small army defeated the Persians at Marathon, twenty-six miles northeast of Athens. From 490 to 481 the Athenians, under Themistocles, built up their navy, and the city became a major sea power.

In 481 the Persians, under Xerxes, began their invasion of Greece. A Greek army, led by Leonidas and about 300 Spartans, fought a desperate battle at Thermopylae, and lost. The Athenians evacuated their city and took refuge on their island of Salamis. In 480 their navy fought a tremendous battle against the Persian navy in the Bay of Salamis, and won. In 479 a combined Greek army led by Athenians and Spartans inflicted a crushing defeat upon the Persians at Plataea. These victories presented the first instance in history of the triumph of quality over quantity, and Athens followed them up with continued pressure on the Persians until every Greek city in the Aegean had been liberated. This war of liberation lasted from 478 to 470, and left Athens the unquestioned mistress of the Aegean. As the cities were liberated they entered into the Delian League, a confederacy which was headed by Athens and which maintained a common treasury on the sacred island of Delos.

GOLDEN AGE OF PERICLES: As the years passed, the policy of Athens changed, and she transformed herself from the pre-

siding state of the Delian League into the sovereign city of a
subject-empire. Her former allies became tributaries who were
prevented by force from withdrawing from the league, the
treasury was moved to Athens, and the internal institutions of
the cities were remodeled in the interest of the Athenian state.
As this was happening Pericles was first elected chief Athenian
general, a position to which he was re-elected many times. He
became the leader of the Ecclesia and the unofficial ruler of
Athens. During his years of leadership (461-429 B.C.) Athenian democracy, culture, and commerce reached their greatest
heights.

ATHENIAN DEMOCRACY UNDER PERICLES: As has been seen,
the Greeks felt that the true life of the citizen was to be found
in service to the state in peace and war, and Pericles strove to
make such a life possible in Athens. According to Thucydides,
the Athenian citizen force numbered 30,200 in 430 B.C. To
this figure must be added about 20,000 males of the lowest
property class, thus giving about 50,000 adult male citizens.
Women, children, and the aged would more than double this
number, giving perhaps 200,000 free persons, plus 50,000 resident aliens, or a total of about 250,000 free Athenians. Only
the 50,000 adult male citizens were able to vote or hold office,
and they also had the right to attend, speak, and vote at the
weekly meetings of the Ecclesia. At the Ecclesia, foreign and
domestic policy and economics were determined, and magistrates elected and their reports examined. All measures were
passed by majority vote. Jurors and other officials were chosen
by lot from among the citizens, a procedure which insured the
principle of rotation in office. Citizens were now paid for their
services to the state, including holding office, serving on juries,
attending the *Ecclesia*, and later even attending the theatre.
This enabled even the poorest citizen to exercise his citizenship
in full, for one of the most important requirements of the citizen was enough leisure to enable him to perform his civic duties.

WOMEN AND EDUCATION UNDER PERICLES: Women were
citizens, but non-voting citizens. They were expected to take
care of the household and supervise the children. Marriages
were arranged by parents, and the woman's dowry was usually
an important factor. If the marriage turned out to be unsatis-
factory the husband could easily divorce his wife by simply re-

turning her dowry; divorce for the wife was almost impossible, however. Primary education, conducted in private schools, was virtually universal for citizens from the age of six to fourteen. The emphasis was upon reading, writing, arithmetic, literature, music, and gymnastics. The primary aim was the development of a sound mind in a sound body as a preparation for good citizenship. The youth became a citizen at the age of eighteen, and then underwent military training until he was twenty.

PELOPONNESIAN WAR—431-404 B.C.: The war pitted the maritime power of Athens against a coalition under the leadership of Sparta. The war was an intermittent affair, waxing and waning according to circumstances. In 430-429 there was a plague at Athens which resulted in the death of Pericles. In 421 the Peace of Nicias was negotiated, but it was soon broken. In 416 the island of Melos was brutally forced to enter the Athenian Empire, the Athenians arguing that necessity knows no law; that political expediency overrides all claims of moral obligations; and that the tyranny of the strong over the weak is the natural right of gods and men. The Athenian navy then went on an expedition to conquer Syracuse, and although the expedition was initially successful, the navy was eventually annihilated (415-413). The resulting gradual attrition forced Athens to surrender finally in 404 B.C. Ironically, the subject-cities that had risen against Athens in the hope of regaining their independence now lay helpless under the yoke of Sparta. Even more ironically, Athens, almost alone of the cities, was later able to shake off the Spartans completely and restore her democracy and trade. But her empire was no more; instead the genius of the city found its true and lasting home in the fields of literature and thought.

THUCYDIDES: The story of the Peloponnesian War was told by Thucydides. His work is a magnificent creation of reflective history. He saw the conflict as a drama which focused and turned on the growing hubris of Athens, culminating in the retribution (nemesis) that resulted when, in the attempt to conquer Syracuse, the city overstepped the mark. Herodotus had portrayed the hand of a jealous Providence in the nemesis that overtook the Persians, when, in their great pride of power, they attempted to conquer Greece; so Thucydides saw, in the catastrophe that befell his own native city, a catastrophe that occurred at the very instant when Athens' thirst for universal empire seemed to have achieved its goal, the inexorable working of the laws that govern and determine the destiny of nations.

RELIGION AND MORALITY: The Greeks worshipped gods who possessed human attributes, such as passion, anger, jealousy, as well as human strengths and weaknesses. At Athens, the principal gods worshipped were Zeus and Athene. Ironically, although the gods were powerful, it was nonetheless believed that they were subject to a superior divine force called Fate. Much attention was paid to ritual prayer and sacrifice, and oracles, omens, and dreams were believed to reveal the will of the gods. There were many religious festivals held throughout Greece, with major ones taking place at Athens. Finally, although it was believed that the soul lived on in Hades, the primary emphasis of the Greek was upon man in this life.

PHILOSOPHY: Fifth-century Greece saw the rise of the Sophists and the birth of Socrates and Plato. Although the term Sophists meant simply "professors of wisdom" (*sophia*), Plato later implied that the wisdom professed was illusory. They trained citizens for success, whether political or financial, in social life through public speaking, and consequently they emphasized clever and tricky methods of arguing on any side of a question, without regard for truth. They were opposed to the traditional religion and morality, and taught scepticism, agnosticism, and rationalism; they were opposed to absolute standards of conduct, and taught relativity in ethics.

They also taught that all individuals and groups are in constant conflict with each other; that life is a never-ending contest for superiority and power; that justice is neither absolute nor impartial, but is the imposed will of the stronger person or group; that self-interest is the primary drive of all; and that laws and customs are not god-made but man-made, and are therefore subject to continual change. "Nothing exists," wrote Gorgias, and, "if it exists it cannot be known by man; if it can be known it cannot be expressed." Protagoras wrote, "Man is the measure of all things," and, "With regard to the gods it is impossible to determine whether they exist or what they are like." And it was Hippias who said, "Religion is a man-made device for enforcing morality through fear," and, "Laws are the conventions of an older generation."

SOCRATES: Socrates lived from 469 to 399 B.C. He was the major opponent of the Sophists, and is considered to be the Father of Ethics. He worried least about the external universe and most about man's inner life and his relations to other men. He attempted to establish standards of conduct that would be absolute, universal, and unchangeable. He taught that happiness depends not on material advantages, but on the perfection of the soul; that virtue is neither enforced nor conventional conduct, but is inner-directed morality based upon reason and understanding; that virtue is knowledge and is teachable and can be learned by reason; and that "Virtue is its own reward." He said, "I am a lover of knowledge, and the men who dwell in the city are my teachers, and not the trees or the country," and he maintained that though he knew nothing else, he did know one thing: his own ignorance. "An unexamined life," he asserted, "is not worth living," and his central teaching to his fellow-citizens was that they should "take care of their souls." He was put to death, at the age of seventy, in 399 B.C. by a thankless city that had passed its prime.

PLATO: Plato was born in 427 and died in 347 B.C. He was Socrates' chief disciple for about ten years, and he was so disillusioned with Athens after the execution of Socrates that he left the city and traveled abroad for about ten years. He returned to Athens and founded the Academy, probably in 388 B.C., the first university in the world, and one which was in existence for almost 900 years. Plato taught that true reality exists in a super-sensory world of intellectual concepts or Ideas which are eternal and unchanging. The material world is made up of shadows of reality, and although these shadows can be perceived by the senses they do not lead to truth, for truth can be reached only by reasoning about Ideas. Indeed, truth might not be reached at all, even in this way, until after death. All Ideas are arranged into a pyramidal hierarchy, with the Idea of Good standing at the apex.

In his theory of the soul, Plato asserted that the soul is the divine and immortal part of a man; that it existed before it entered the body, and that it retains memories of its association with Ideas; and that after the death of the body, the soul again enters the realm of pure Ideas. Agreeing with Socrates, Plato said that virtue is knowledge; that only wisdom can bring happiness, which is almost entirely intellectual; and that physical pleasures should be shunned because they hinder the pursuit of wisdom. He also said that love is yearning after perfect Beauty, Truth, and Goodness. Regarding government and society, Plato condemned democracy, oligarchy, and despotism, and advocated an ideal commonwealth based on justice, ruled by philosopher-kings, defended and maintained by soldiers, and supported by workers. He also urged equality of women, compulsory education, didacticism in art and literature, and the universal brotherhood of man. With the death of Plato the fading glory of fifth-century Athens dimmed irrevocably and went out.

THE DEVELOPMENT OF GREEK DRAMA

The beginnings of drama, in virtually all places and times, have been closely bound up with religion and ritual. This was particularly true of Greek drama, which almost literally developed out of ritual into art. Songs and dances in honor of Dionysus, god of wine and vegetation and symbol of creative power, were performed quite early in Greece, as a part of an annual religious ceremony in honor of the god. There were five major aspects to the ceremony: prayer, procession, phallic symbol, dithyramb, and sacrifice.

THE PROCESSION: The entire ceremony centered on the offering of the sacrifice. Originally a human being was the victim, but later a goat (*tragos*) was substituted. The object of the procession was to convey the animal solemnly to the place where it would be sacrificed. At first a statue of Dionysus was carried in the procession, but later a man represented him. The god was depicted as a long-haired, bearded man; two short horns projected from his forehead, symbolizing his energy; he had a crown of ivy on his head and a staff entwined with leaves and surmounted by a pine cone in his hand to symbolize that his power of action was not affected by the change of seasons; and a huge phallus, symbolic of his creative power, was carried in front of him in a basket. In front of the god walked virgins crowned with garlands, and behind him went a group of Bacchantes variously costumed as satyrs (animals with the head of a man and the legs of a goat), in goatskins; inebriates, with their faces and garments smeared with wine; and spirits from Hades, with white lead or horrifying death masks covering their faces.

DITHYRAMBS: After the procession had reached the place of sacrifice, and while the animal was being prepared, *dithyrambs* were performed in honor of the god by a chorus of fifty men

23

dressed as goats. These dithyrambs were leaping dances, or dances of abandonment, accompanied by dramatic movements, the music of flutes, and appropriate hymns relating to the life of Dionysus. A story about Dionysus was often improvised by the leader of the chorus, who sometimes dressed as a character from mythology. Since the word for goat was tragos, the popular name for a satyr was tragos (goat); the chorus was called the tragic, or goat-chorus, and the dithyramb was called the tragic, or goat-song. Thus what we call Greek tragedy is a direct outcome of the chorus, and although the satyr chorus underwent much change as tragedy developed, it remained in virtually its original form in what came to be called the satyr play, changing only its name to the satyric chorus.

THE KOMOS: As time went on a lighter element was added to the Bacchantic procession: a number of enthusiastic worshippers of Dionysus and the phallic symbol who were not a part of the official escort of the god but who were more than just ordinary spectators. In a gay group, called a *komos*, they went through the town singing songs in honor of the phallus and joking with the crowd. At first the songs were improvised, but later they were rehearsed before being performed by a chorus of the young men. From the name of the group, komos, the chorus was called the comic chorus, and its songs were called comedies.

TRAGEDY AND COMEDY: It is worth noting that while the tragedy and satyr plays were integral parts of divine worship and therefore treated of supernatural beings, fates, and events, the comedy was nothing but an exchange of wit with the object of touching one another's weak points without anyone giving the impression of being offended, no matter how deeply he might really have felt hurt. This essential difference was maintained as drama continued to develop, with tragedy continuing to present the lives of gods and heroes, while comedy still attacked contemporary follies and the events of everyday life.

THESPIS: Very little is definitely known about Thespis, but much is attributed to him; consequently he is called the Father of the Drama. He lived in the sixth century (c.550-500 B.C.), and was a teacher of the chorus. He may have been the first, or at least one of the first, to break with tradition by inserting hero-legends into the Bacchic dithyrambs. He seems also to have portrayed the heroes themselves as living and speaking with the leader of the chorus. Thus were born the first actor (*hypokrites*, or answerer), and the first drama, or action. Horace, who tells of Thespis in his *Ars Poetica*, also credits the innovator with the idea of changing masks to match the person being portrayed. In 535 B.C. Thespis, who was not an Athenian, was invited by Pisistratus, the Athenian tyrant, to bring his tragedies to Athens, and he was apparently the first to win a prize for his productions in that city. None of his dramas have survived. From his name, of course, has come our word *thespian*.

DRAMATIC CHANGES: In the fifth century, Aeschylus added a second actor and reduced the chorus to twelve, and a generation later Sophocles added a third actor and raised the chorus to fifteen, the figure at which it remained. There were never more than three actors in a drama, though there were usually more than three solo parts. One actor would usually portray the central character, while each of the others would play many of the lesser roles. The chorus, although almost always an integral part of a Greek drama, gradually declined in importance as the dialogue became increasingly prominent.

PLAY PRODUCTION: Dramatic productions were always confined to the great festivals of Dionysus, and they were regarded as a religious ceremonial, an act of homage to the god. There were three such festivals: the Great (or City) Dionysia, which occupied five days at the end of March; the Lenaea, which took place at the end of January, and at which either comedies or tragedies might be performed; and the Rural Dionysia, which took place at the end of December. The Great Dionysia was a tremendous holiday: business ceased, the law courts were closed, debts were forgiven, and prisoners were released from jail. Usually at this time the allies sent their annual tribute to Athens, and many ambassadors were on hand to transact diplomatic business. In addition, large numbers of strangers were attracted by the celebrity of the festival. Aeschines, the rhetorician, described the audience in the theatre at the City Dionysia as consisting of the "whole Greek nation."

Since dramatic performances were sacred institutions in honor of Dionysus they were entirely in the hands of the state. An *archon* (magistrate) was responsible for the superintending of them. He had to select the poets and approve their plays, appoint the *choregus* (the man who paid the expenses) for each poet, and arrange for the actors.

SELECTION OF POETS AND CHOREGI: When a poet wished to compete in one of the festivals he sent his application and copies of the plays he wished to present to the archon. The archon read all the plays submitted and then chose the required number of poets. This number varied in accordance with the festival: three for the City Dionysia; two for the Lenaea, unless comedies were being performed, in which case the number would be either three or five. After the poet was chosen he was provided with a choregus. The choregus was always one of the wealthier citizens of Athens, for, as has been noted, he had to pay for the training and costuming of the chorus. This was a public responsibility, provided for by law, which was normally undertaken by rotation. The poets and choregi were paired by lot in order to prevent the exercising of favoritism. The actors now remained to be chosen, and the process of their selection varied at different periods.

Prior to Aeschylus only one actor was needed in each play, and his part was taken by the poet. When Aeschylus added a second actor, tragedy was converted from a chiefly lyrical to a primarily dramatic form of art. Poets stopped acting in their own plays, and thus the actor's profession came into being. For about fifty years the poets chose their own actors, and particular actors were often permanently associated with particular poets. About the middle of the fifth century contests in acting were established, and the selection of the actors was taken out of the hands of the poets. The archon selected three protagonists, who then chose their own one or two subordinate actors. Once the three leading actors had been named, they were assigned to the poets by lot. This means of selection was basically the same for both tragedy and comedy.

TRAINING OF THE CHORUS: The choregus now had to hire the members of the chorus, usually from the general body of citizens, though later a class of professional singers sprang up. In addition to paying these singers, the choregus also had to provide them with a room in which to practice, and a special diet so that they would be in the best possible condition for the competition. Plutarch mentions eels, lettuce, garlic, and cheese as some of the delicacies provided for this latter purpose. Although the choregus had to pay the expenses of training the chorus, the training itself was at first undertaken by the poet, with the aid of an assistant. By the end of the fifth century, however, this training was entirely in the hands of a professional instructor. The choregus also had to hire a flute player and various characters who were not a part of the chorus, had no lines, but nonetheless appeared on the stage as, for example, attendants upon kings and queens.

The costumes provided by the choregus for all of the members of the cast were always expensive and often very magnificent. Aristophanes, for instance, mentions the case of a choregus who ruined himself financially by outfitting his chorus in gold. Since the competition between poets, major actors, and choregi was intense, each choregus tried to outdo the others, and this naturally increased the expense. It would seem that from $1,500 to $3,000 might be spent by a choregus for the privilege of producing four plays for one performance only, since the same play was not presented again in Athens. The choregus received no payment from the state, and only one of the three could win the prize, which consisted of a wreath of ivy.

THE AWARDING OF PRIZES: Similar prizes were awarded to the victorious poet and chief actor. The recipients of these prizes were determined partly by judges and partly by lot. There were ten judges, all Athenian citizens, who were themselves chosen by lot. The order in which the plays were to be performed was also chosen in this manner. After the competition the judges inscribed their verdicts on tablets, five of which were then chosen, again by lot, and those five decided the result. Although the wreaths themselves were of no particular value, they represented some of the highest honors that could be bestowed upon an Athenian by his fellow citizens.

THE TETRALOGY: Each of the three poets was required to present four plays: three tragedies and one satyr play. The four plays were called a *tetralogy*, and usually dealt with different aspects of the same legend. Later the tragedies, instead of dealing with a unified theme, often were on separate subjects, and the satyr play usually included Dionysus among its characters, as a reminder to the audience that the festival was in his honor. The three tragedies were called a *trilogy*.

DAILY PERFORMANCES: The audience usually entered the theatre at daybreak, and went prepared to stay until sundown. Usually five plays were produced each day: a tetralogy and one comedy, although occasionally a second comedy was performed. Three comic poets, who presented one play each, also competed for a prize. The audience ate a hearty breakfast and also took provisions along to the theatre. They would sometimes work off energy during the long day's proceedings by applauding or censuring the actors and by throwing things, ranging from flowers to rocks as the situation demanded. Fairly often actors were pelted with fruit, and there is a case on record of an actor being nearly stoned to death. The festival of Dionysus was a lively one.

ACTORS: As has been stated, the poet originally performed the leading role, but after the second and third actors were added they were all hired by the state. The actors were all men, as were the members of the chorus, though the latter might at times be made up of boys. With the exception of the chief actor, who was called the protagonist, each actor usually performed more than one role. The extras, who played such parts as attendants, have already been mentioned. There were never more than three actors in any Greek drama.

COSTUME—MASKS: Greek dramatic costume, as it was standardized in the fifth century, had three outstanding features: the mask; the *cothurnus*, a high-soled boot; and the tunic and mantle. The masks were usually made of linen covered with plaster, though cork and wood were sometimes used, and they covered the entire head, front and back. On the tragic mask the main traits of the character represented were depicted in bold and striking lines which exaggerated every feature and gave superhuman dignity and terror to the expression. The satyric masks were much the same, but the comic masks were not. When real personages were portrayed in comedies, the masks were portraits of the actual persons. The fictitious comic masks, however, were grotesque and extravagant, with the mouth large and wide open and the features twisted into a grimace. The mouth of the tragic mask was also wide open, a feature which evidently added resonance to the actor's voice, a matter of some importance in the large, open-air Greek theatre.

There were two other characteristic features of the tragic mask:

the *onkos*, and the wig. The onkos was a cone-shaped projection from the upper part of the mask above the forehead, designed to give size and impressiveness to the face. The onkos was used when dignity was to be conveyed, and it varied in size in accordance with the character of the personage being portrayed. The wig was an integral part of the mask, and it, together with the height of the onkos, the color of the complexion, and the expression of the eyes, was used to discriminate one type of character from another. For example, the tyrant had black hair, the handsome youth fair ringlets, and the aged lady white hair.

COTHURNUS: The cothurnus, or tragic boot, was a boot with a wooden sole of varying thickness attached to it. The intention was to increase the height of the actors, thereby giving them an appearance of superhuman grandeur. The thickness of the sole varied in accordance with the dignity and position of the wearer. The cothurnus was rarely if ever worn by satyric actors, and never by comic actors.

TUNIC AND MANTLE: The tragic actor wore garments equivalent to ordinary Greek clothes, differing only in their style, color, and magnificence. These were an undergarment, or tunic, and an overgarment, or mantle. The tunic was brilliantly colored, adorned with stripes, animals, flowers, or similar designs, and reached to the actor's feet. Queens wore tunics of purple, or of white trimmed with purple, which usually trailed on the ground. The tunic flowed down in long and graceful folds, giving an appearance of height and dignity. There were two types of mantle: the *himation* and the *chlamys*. The himation was a long mantle which went over the right shoulder and covered most of the body. The chlamys was a short cloak draped over the left shoulder. Mantles were also brightly colored. Satyric and comic actors wore similar mantles except that the tunics were somewhat shorter.

COMIC COSTUMES: The costumes of the comic actors differed from those of the tragic and satyric actors in several ways not already mentioned. The phallus was regularly worn, and Aristophanes was apparently the first to eliminate it completely in some of his plays. The figures of the actors were grotesquely padded, front and back, into a completely ludicrous shape. The padding was enclosed in a tight-fitting undergarment which covered all of the actor's body except his head, hands, and feet. The garment itself was made of an elastic knitted material so it would fit close to the body, and it was usually dyed a flesh color to represent the skin. Finally, the tunics and mantles worn by the comic actors seem to have been shorter than those worn in ordinary life so that the phallus could be displayed.

CHORIC COSTUMES: The costumes of the chorus were quite different from those of the actors. The tragic, satyric, and comic choruses all wore masks, but that was their only similarity. The tragic chorus was usually composed of old men, or women, or maidens, and the masks were appropriate to those being represented. The tunics and mantles were those of ordinary dress, for the tragic chorus was generally supposed to represent the ordinary public. The satyric chorus was supposed to represent satyrs, so the members wore goats horns, hoofs, and tails. The tail was attached to a kind of loincloth from which the inevitable phallus was also hung. Flesh-colored full-length tights were worn to indicate that the satyrs were naked.

The chorus of the Old Comedy was by far the most fanciful and varied. When poets, sophists, athletes, sorcerers, knights, and the like were portrayed, they were dressed in the tunic and mantle of everyday life. When furies, Amazons, sphinxes, sirens, or other mythological beings were depicted they appeared in the appropriate traditional costume. When there were such choruses as towns, islands, clouds, dramas, and seasons, the costumer usually tried only remotely to indicate the ideas or objects because of the difficulties involved. There was also some difficulty when the chorus was composed of birds, wasps, frogs, storks, ants, fish, bees, and the like. The major part of these costumes seems to have extended from the waist to the head, leaving the legs free for dancing.

THE CHORUS: A number of important functions were performed by the chorus. It often set the mood and presented the central themes of the drama. It also interpreted many of the events as they took place, thereby acting as a bridge between the actors and the audience. At the same time it gave much background information, thus informing the audience of the important events that had taken place prior to the time depicted in the play. Finally, the chorus conversed with and often gave advice to the major characters in the play, advice which, ironically enough, was almost never heeded, and never in time. The chorus used song, speech, and recitative, depending upon the meter used, and most of the choral songs were accompanied by dances, the purpose of which was to represent various objects and events by means of gestures, postures and attitudes.

Each of the three different kinds of drama had its own particular kind of dance. The tragic dance was called the *emmeleia*, and was grave and majestic in its motions. The satyric dance was called the *sikinnis*. It was mainly a parody and caricature of noble and graceful dances, and it was quite rapid and violent in its movements. The comic dance was called the *kordax*. It was coarse and lascivious, suggestive of the phallic songs out of which comedy had developed. It was a dance for drunken people, for only a man with no sense of shame would dance it when he was sober. As has previously been stated, Aeschylus reduced the size of the chorus from fifty to twelve, and Sophocles raised it to fifteen. At all times, however, there was one member of the chorus who was also the leader, a position that was quite arduous. While the dialogue was in progress the leader, representing the chorus, had to carry on conversations with the actors. During the choral odes he had to give the note to the rest of the chorus and supervise the dances and maneuvers, and at the same time his own dancing and gestures were supposed to be a conspicuous feature of the performance.

THE FORM OF TRAGEDY: The typical Greek tragedy has very distinct sections: *prologos, parodos, episode, stasimon,* and *exodos.* The prologos (prologue) is an introductory scene in which the principal actor (protagonist) gives his opening speech. The prologue is usually an integral part of the play and serves the purpose of setting the scene and presenting the situation in the drama. The parodos follows; this is the entrance lyric by the chorus. Then comes a dramatic scene (episode), and a stasimon, or choral ode. A tragedy eventually came to have five episodes separated by choral odes. In the final scene, in which the action is concluded, a messenger may report the catastrophe or a god may be brought onto the stage to resolve the complications and throw light on future events. Then, usually, the chorus delivers its final lines and leaves (exodos).

The choral odes were written in a variety of meters, and were sung and danced to and had a flute accompaniment. The choral

ode, or stasimon, was antiphonal: it consisted of a "turn" and
"counterturn," or "movement" and "counter-movement," of a
series of lines constituting a *strophe* followed by an *antistrophe*
of the same length and metrical form. Quite often the strophe
was sung by one half of the chorus, and the antistrophe was the
answer sung by the second half. There might also be an *epode*,
or combined finale. Sometimes, in place of a stasimon there
was a *kommos*, which consisted of alternating passages of dialogue between the protagonist and the chorus, and later, in
plays of Euripides, a solo song was substituted for a stasimon.

THE FORM OF OLD COMEDY: The typical Greek comedy
opens with a prologos in which the leading character conceives
an unusual plan, or "happy idea," such as staging a sex strike
or going down to Hades to bring back a dead poet because all
the living ones are mediocre. The chorus, decked out fantasti-
cally in costumes suggestive of practically anything (wasps,
frogs, clouds, birds) makes its entrance with a song (parodos).
Episodes present the application and working-out of the plan.
Part way through the play there is an *agon*. This is a debate
between a proponent and opponent of the plan. This continues
until the proponent defeats his rival, usually with a torrent of
off-color argument and vituperation. Usually the agon is immediately followed by the *parabasis*, a scene in which the chorus delivers a long and highly charged harangue, voicing the
poet's views on a large variety of subjects.

THE GREEK THEATRE

DEVELOPMENT OF THE THEATRE: The Greek theatre developed as a natural outgrowth of the Dionysian festivals. When the performances and sacrifices central to the festivals took place on the sacred ground near the temple of Dionysus, the sacrificial altar, or *thymele*, became the focal point of the activities. Around this altar, on bare ground which had been stamped hard and flat, the chorus of Bacchus performed its dances. The limit of this performing area was marked by a limestone circle, and this circular space with the altar at the center was called the *orchestra*. Since everyone in the region wished to see the dances and hear the songs, it became the custom to locate the orchestra in a place surrounded by hills so that the more distant spectators could view the performance. As time went on, the festivals lasted longer and the demand for comfort increased; consequently, scaffoldings with wooden benches were built on the slopes surrounding the orchestra so that the public might watch the sacred activities with a minimum of fatigue. By the end of the sixth century B.C. the form of the Greek theatre was firmly fixed.

THEATRICAL CHANGES: The fifth century, which saw the full flowering of Greek drama, also saw a number of developments and modifications in the theatre. One of these was the result of a theatrical accident. During a dramatic performance in Athens, in which Aeschylus was one of the competitors, the scaffolding collapsed, causing a considerable number of injuries and deaths. After this the *theatron*, or auditorium, was enlarged and the space under the seats filled in with dirt. The seats, which were actually benches, were still placed in circular rows around the orchestra, and they were always of wood. There were no stone benches in Greek theatres until the fourth century. The orchestra, which was also called the stage, remained basically what it had been, namely, a circular dancing place with an altar in the middle of it. The fifth century theatre in

33

Athens was a large one; it was able to accommodate about 17,000 spectators.

THEATRICAL BUILDINGS: For a considerable length of time the altar was the only fixed and permanent structure on or near the orchestra, but during the time of Aeschylus and by the time of Sophocles a building, called the *skene*, was added. The skene was, in effect, a dressing room. In it the actors and chorus put on their costumes before the performance began, and the actors retired to it during the performance to change costumes when necessary. It was probably Sophocles who caused the skene to be built at the rear of the orchestra so that it could play a part in the productions. A decorative facade, called the *proscenium*, was then built in front of the skene, touching the edge of the orchestra. The proscenium was about ten to twelve feet high, and its most prominent feature was a row of pillars at its front. Later a wing, called a *parascenium*, projecting toward the orchestra, was added at either side of the proscenium. Many uses were made by Greek dramatists of the proscenium, which could become a temple, a palace, a wall, or whatnot, as well as of the roofs of the proscenium, skene, and parascenia, which were flat.

On either side of the skene there was a *parodos*, or entrance, by which the spectators entered the theatre and the chorus came on the stage. The actors also used these parodoi if they were not supposed to come out of the skene through the proscenium.

THEATRICAL MACHINERY: There were three significant mechanical devices used in the Greek theatre: the *eccyclema*, the *mechane*, and the *theologeion*.

ECCYCLEMA: The eccyclema was a small wooden platform on wheels, which was normally kept inside the skene. Because in the Greek theatre the action always took place in the open air, in front of a temple, palace, or the like, and because it was impossible to transfer the action to the inside of the building due to the continual presence of the chorus on stage, plus the facts that the skene was too narrow to be used, and even if it were deeper a good part of the audience would not be able to see into it, interior action, if its showing were desired to produce a powerful dramatic effect, had to be brought out onto the orchestra. At these times one of the doors of the skene would be opened and the eccyclema pushed out. On it would be a group of figures, representing in a kind of tableau the deed or occurrence which had just taken place inside the building. The eccyclema was chiefly used in situations where a murder had been committed, and the tableau would present the corpse or corpses, and the murderer or murderers standing or crouched with the bloody weapons in hand.

MECHANE: The mechane, or "machine," was a sort of crane with a pulley attached, by which weights could be raised or lowered. It was located at the top left-hand side of the skene. It was used when the characters of a play had to appear or disappear in a supernatural manner. By means of the mechane a god or hero could be lowered from heaven down to earth, or raised from earth to heaven, or even be held suspended in mid-air. Sometimes the character was shown sitting in a chariot or on a winged steed, but usually he was simply suspended from the rope by means of a hook and bands fastened around his body. The mechane was obviously quite strong, since it sometimes had to support two or three people at one time. The use of the mechane ultimately gave rise to the expression *deus ex machina*, or "god from the machine."

THEOLOGEION: The theologeion was a narrow, movable platform on the top of the skene, similar in construction to the eccyclema. It was also used to exhibit gods in a supernatural manner, but on it the gods were represented as stationary in heaven rather than moving through the air.

THE SUPPLIANT MAIDENS

(circa 490 B.C.)

BACKGROUND: *The Suppliant Maidens* is generally considered to be the earliest extant Greek drama, and is commonly thought to have been first produced in about 490 B.C. A recently discovered papyrus seems to indicate, however, that this play was not produced until after 470. If this is correct, then it would appear that Aeschylus wrote the play about twenty years before he staged it, for the style of *The Suppliant Maidens* is quite archaic compared to that of *The Persians*, which was produced in 472. Irrespective of which play was produced first, it seems apparent that *The Suppliant Maidens* remains the oldest surviving Greek drama written. This play was probably the first drama of a tetralogy of which the other plays no longer exist. They evidently were *The Egyptians*, *The Daughters of Danaus*, and *Amymone*, a satyr-play.

The Suppliant Maidens is of great historical interest because it represents a period of transition between the original lyric dithyramb and classical dramatic tragedy. The chorus here probably has fifty members, as in the original dithyramb, and is the protagonist. About one-half of the play consists of choral lyrics. There are two actors, an innovation of Aeschylus', and that this is an early instance of the use of the second actor is indicated by the awkwardness with which he is employed. For a fuller discussion of Greek drama and the use of additional actors, see the chapter on the development of Greek drama. There are a few other dramatic problems in the play that might be noted. There is little action, little characterization, entirely too much geographical and genealogical detail, and the preponderance of lyric makes it primarily a choral rather than a dramatic work. All of these tend to make *The Suppliant Maidens* an interesting, but not very dramatic, play.

THEMES: Because the other two plays of the trilogy are lost and the exact meaning of certain passages of *The Suppliant Maidens* is difficult to determine definitely due to the corruptness of the text, Aeschylus' exact purpose is uncertain. However, the major theme of this play, as an individual play, would seem to be the dilemma in which King Pelasgus finds himself: should he grant the right of sanctuary even though this may result in war, or should he refuse the suppliants and have the altars of his gods polluted with their blood? The overall theme of the trilogy as a whole would seem to center on the conflict between endogamy, or marriage within a family or tribal group, and exogamy, or marriage outside of those groups, and that problem is certainly present in *The Suppliant Maidens*. Secondary themes include the conflicts between primitive and civilized attitudes of thought and behavior, the innate male-female hostility as opposed to the innate male-female attraction, as well as the conflicts between violence and reason, tribal law and civic law, and individual freedom and obedience to a higher authority, secular or divine.

LEGEND: The general story is different in a number of ways from Aeschylus' version, so it is easy to see why interpretation of his drama is difficult. It seems that Zeus fell in love with Io, one of Hera's Argive priestesses. (This story is referred to in considerable detail in Aeschylus' *Prometheus Bound*.) Hera became quite jealous; she transformed Io into a cow and made her undergo many torments. Finally, Zeus by "touching" Io, changed her back into a mortal, and she gave birth to Epaphus, who became the father of Libya, who in her turn bore twin sons, Belus and Agenor. Belus later became the father of another pair of twin sons, Aegyptus and Danaus. Aegyptus ruled over Arabia and Egypt, and had fifty sons; Danaus ruled Libya, and had fifty daughters.

After Belus' death, his two sons quarrelled, and Aegyptus finally proposed a mass marriage between their children. Danaus' suspicions of foul play were confirmed by an oracle which asserted that Aegyptus planned to kill Danaus' daughters (the Danaids), and with them he fled to Argos, where he claimed the kingdom and received it. Aegyptus thereupon sent his sons there with orders not to return until they had punished Danaus and his family. When they arrived they implored Danaus to allow them to marry his daughters, intending to slaughter them on the wedding night. Danaus finally agreed, himself planning to have his nephews killed on the same night. To achieve this, he gave either fifty sharp pins or fifty daggers to his daughters, and at midnight each one, with the sole exception of Hypermnestra, stabbed her husband through the heart.

Hypermnestra, moved by a combination of love and pity, and the fact that her spouse, Lynceus, had spared her maidenhead, could not bring herself to convert Lynceus from a strong, vigorous, living young man to a cold and dead one, so she woke him, told him what had happened to his brothers, and helped him to escape. Danaus, after he learned of his daughter's disobedience, first imprisoned her, and then put her on trial for her life. A jury of Argive judges, partly through the intercession of Aphrodite, acquitted her, and Hypermnestra subsequently caused a statue of the goddess to be placed in the shrine of Apollo at Argos. The Danaids were eventually purified by Athene and Hermes, but even so, after their deaths they were condemned to the never-ending task of carrying water in jars perforated with holes. Hypermnestra and Lynceus were later reunited, after which Lynceus killed Danaus in revenge and himself reigned over Argos.

CHARACTERS:

CHORUS OF MAIDENS   Daughters of Danaus.

DANAUS   Their father.

PELASGUS   King of Argos.

HERALD   Sent by Aegyptus, King of Egypt and brother of Danaus.

ATTENDANTS   Mute parts.

SETTING: The action takes place at a sacred grove near Argos. There are a number of statues of Greek gods and a large central altar.

COMMENT: The altar is the altar of Dionysus, which was at the center of the orchestra of all Greek theatres.

PROLOGUE AND PARODOS: Danaus, together with his fifty

daughters, who comprise the Chorus, enter, wearing rich, Oriental-style costumes, and carrying the wands of suppliants. The Chorus prays to Zeus to protect them in their flight from their cousins, insolent men who want to force them into marriage against their will, and calls upon Io, their ancestress by Zeus, and her son Epaphus to hear and aid them, also. Their continuing laments, they say, will be so loud and plaintive that passersby will think they hear the bird-cries of Philomela. They hope that Zeus' will toward them, dark and inscrutable as it is, will be favorable. They invoke the protector of the Apian land to give them shelter and protection in their plight, remarking on the many times they have rent their Sidonian veils in grief. Finally, they ask Artemis to help them to remain virgins. If not, they say, they will hang themselves and appeal in death to Zeus for Justice.

COMMENT: Zeus is the first god appealed to by the Danaids because he is the lord of the gods, he is the protector of travelers, and he is their ancestor through Io. Their prayer to Io and Epaphus is also based on the fact that the Danaids are their descendants. Artemis, daughter of Zeus and Leto, and twin sister of Apollo, was one of the three virgin goddesses (the other two being Athene and Hestia). She was goddess of the hunt and of the moon. She was known as the proud virgin, and it is obvious why the Chorus, desirous of preserving their virginity, call upon her for help.

The wands carried by the members of the Chorus are olive branches, traditionally carried by suppliants. The clothes of the Chorus, and of Danaus, are significant, for they are quite obviously not Greek, but Oriental. Greek clothes were not splendid in appearance, but were rather plain and simple. The Chorus' reference to their tearing of their Sidonian veils points this contrast up, for Sidon was a city on the Mediterranean northeast of Egypt, thus an Oriental city. For a further discussion of Greek clothing, see the chapter on the development of the Greek theatre.

Apis was an Egyptian and Libyan bull-god with whom Epaphus became associated. Zeus, as the ancestor of Epaphus, who in turn was the ancestor of the rulers of Egypt and Libya, is therefore being invoked as the protector of the land of Apis, which includes the Danaids' home from which they have fled. Philomela was the sister of Procne, who was the wife of Tereus, King of Thrace. Tereus became enamored of Philomela, hid Procne in a cabin after cutting out her tongue, and married the younger sister. Procne conveyed the story to her sister by weaving it into a robe, and Philomela released her. Procne gained revenge by killing her son, boiling him, and serving his flesh to his father. When Tereus realized what he had been eating, he siezed an axe to kill Procne and Philomela. The gods, however, changed all three into birds: Tereus became a hoopoe, Procne a swallow, and Philomela a nightingale. The Chorus, therefore, is equating its laments with those of Philomela, who was herself an unwilling and dishonored bed-mate of a man she did not really want.

FIRST EPISODE: Danaus, who has been standing quietly by during his daughters' invocations, now advises prudence, for he sees armed men in chariots approaching. Since these are probably the rulers of the country, it would be wise for them to act as the suppliants they are, using the altar as a shield as they tell their sorrowful story to the newcomers. The Chorus again invokes the gods, all of whom are worshipped at this common altar, and waits patiently. Pelasgus, King of Argos, enters, followed by his attendants and soldiers, and immediately asks who these barbarians are, who are dressed in barbaric and luxurious clothes. The Chorus, before answering, desires to know who it is speaking to. Pelasgus names himself and outlines the geographical boundaries of his realm. The Chorus then claims kinship with the Argives, and Pelasgus, in wonder, replies that they seem more like Libyans, Cyprians, or Amazons than they do Argives. In an exchange of lines the Chorus outlines its lineage from Io, who was one of Hera's priestesses in Argos when Zeus began to desire her, and Pelasgus asks why they left their father's home to seek support at Argos. They say they do not want to be household slaves to Aegyptus' sons, and Pelasgus asks if this is the result of their own hatred of their cousins or if the law forbade their marriage to them. The former, they say, and they ask his help in preventing Aegyptus' sons from marrying them. Pelasgus replies that though the gods seem to support his defense of the Danaids, nonetheless it might bring war with Aegyptus. Therefore, he is not qualified to render a decision without asking the citizens of Argos. This is especially true, he says, since Egyptian law prevents the Danaids from legally refusing to marry their cousins; while, on the other hand, he desires to respect the religious rights of suppliants. The Chorus replies that Zeus weighs the just and the unjust, rewarding the former and punishing the latter; why, then, does Pelasgus fear to act justly? He answers that he will not risk bringing destruction upon his city, through the giving of aid to foreigners, without the approval of the citizens. Seeing Pelasgus still indecisive, the Danaids threaten to hang themselves from the statues of the gods that surround the altar if he does not defend them. The king urges Danaus to go into the city dressed as a sea captain, and plead his case to the Argive people. Possibly they will agree to be kind to the suppliants. Danaus leaves, and Pelasgus directs the Chorus to wait while he, too, goes into the city to help their father speak to the people.

COMMENT: Pelasgus apparently enters in a horse-drawn chariot, and his men no doubt carry shields and spears. Also, it is likely that his entrance is heralded by trumpets. All of this is an indication of Aeschylus' love of spectacle. The major themes of the drama are given their first major expression in this Episode. The conflict between endogamy and exogamy is stated by Pelasgus. He does not see how the Danaids could be justified in refusing to marry their cousins since Egyptian law is against them. They must, therefore, marry within their family. They appeal, however, to a higher law, one which might not necessarily allow them to choose which man to marry, but would allow them to choose not to marry a particular suitor. And they offer a particularly good reason for not wanting to marry their cousins, namely, they hate them. It is true that except to say that they would become slaves in their cousins' households they present no substantial basis for their hatred, but even unsubstantiated hatred would hardly be conducive to a satisfactory marriage.

Pelasgus is faced with a tragic dilemma, which forms the other major theme: if he refuses the Danaids his support they will pollute the sacred grove of his city by committing suicide in it, and he himself will be violating hospitality and the religious rights of the suppliant; if he does help them he will undoubtedly involve his city in a war with the Egyptians. The Danaids' argument that when faced with a dilemma such as this the choice must be in favor of the best, most positive, and most just alternative is a sound one, for, as they say, Zeus weighs delicate choices of good and evil and always supports the just. Therefore, in choosing the just alternative (protecting the Danaids), Pelasgus can look forward to Zeus' support even if the Egyptians do make war, but in choosing the unjust alternative, he would bring down upon himself and his city Zeus' anger and enmity.

FIRST STASIMON: The members of the chorus pray again to Zeus, reminding him of their descent from Io. He supported her in her wanderings, they say, and by his touch in Egypt not only changed her back to her womanly form, but also made her the mother of Epaphus. They ask him to watch over them as he watched over her.

COMMENT: This play is interpreted by some as a presentation of the mystical relationship between the gods and mankind. The "touching" of Io by Zeus is at the heart of that interpretation. The depiction in Genesis of God "breathing" life into Adam is a similar type of representation of that mystical relationship.

SECOND EPISODE: Danaus returns from the city and tells the Chorus that the citizens, after hearing what he and Pelasgus had to say, voted their support and protection of the suppliants, even if war should be the result. Through the people of Argo, he says, the will of Zeus has been shown.

COMMENT: This Episode contains another reference to the mystical relationship between gods and men, for Zeus, while not directly interfering, nonetheless has manifested his will through the Argives.

SECOND STASIMON: The Chorus shows its appreciation for the decision of the Argives by asking Zeus to protect the city from war, famine, and plague, and to bring it the fullness of harvests, good government, and honor.

COMMENT: Aeschylus neatly balances the Chorus' first three, essentially negative requests, with its second three, essentially positive ones.

THIRD EPISODE: Danaus tells the Chorus that he has just sighted the Egyptian ships approaching. The Danaids are fearful of their arrogant, unholy, jackal-like cousins, but Danaus says that the Argives will help them as they promised. The Danaids are to wait as suppliants at the sacred grove, he tells them, while he goes to the city for aid.

> **COMMENT:** The Chorus' description of their cousins is further indication, and possibly justification, of their hatred of them.

THIRD STASIMON: The Chorus loudly bewails the coming of the fierce and heartless Egyptians, their cousins, and wish they could make themselves invisible. They swear to kill themselves before gracing the marriage beds of such violent and lustful men, and they call again upon Zeus for protection.

> **COMMENT:** The following Episode fully justifies the Danaids' hatred and horror of their cousins.

FOURTH EPISODE: The Herald of Aegyptus enters, accompanied by attendants. The Danaids cry out for help against the ravishers, and cling to the altar. The Herald calls upon them to go to the boats peacefully or they will be dragged to them forcibly, running the risk of having their heads cut off as well. The Danaids resist, and say they wish the Egyptians had all perished rounding the cape of Sarpedon's tomb. The Herald ignores them, and with his men begins to carry the Danaids off to the ships. The Chorus calls upon the gods whose statues adorn the sacred grove for assistance, but the Herald points out that these are not Egyptian gods and he and his men need have no fear of them. Suddenly Pelasgus arrives with his men and orders the Herald and his men to leave Argos. The Herald claims his right to take away the Danaids, invoking Hermes the Searcher, but Pelasgus points out that though he invokes the gods he shows no reverence to them. Pelasgus again orders the Herald and his men to leave, and the Herald, asserting that this act will bring about war between Egypt and Argos, obeys. Pelasgus then invites the Danaids to enter the city, where homes will be provided for them. They thank him, and again pray for good things to descend upon Argos, and Pelasgus leaves for the city with his men. Danaus enters, coming from the city with additional soldiers. He urges his daughters to give thanks for their deliverance and to live upright and just lives in Argos so as not to bring dishonor upon themselves and him and joy to their cousins. For, he says, tongues are always ready to defame strangers and aliens, and they must scc to it that they give no cause for the utterance of slanders against them. The Danaids promise to behave honorably, and they prepare to enter the city.

> **COMMENT:** Sarpedon was a son of Zeus and Europa who became king of Lycia, in Asia Minor. He died, and was buried there on a promontory. The Danaids wish the Egyptians had been shipwrecked at that point in their voyage to Argos. There is intense irony in the fact, alluded to by Pelasgus, that men who claim to be under the protection of one of the gods, Hermes, should at that precise moment be defiling a grove and altar sacred to other gods by attempting to forcibly drag suppliants away from it. This is another indication of the barbarity of the Egyptians, and further justification of the Danaids' hatred of them. It is interesting that Hermes, messenger of the gods and protector of travelers (hence searchers), was also the god of thieves and cheats. The Herald and his men are here attempting to steal the Danaids. The awkwardness of the entrances and exits, resulting from the limitation of only two actors, should be noted.

FOURTH STASIMON AND EXODOS: The Chorus divides into two parts and sings praises to Argos, their new home. They pray to Artemis that they may never be forced to marry, but they also realize that Aphrodite might will otherwise. All really rests with Zeus, whose mind cannot be read by mortals. They counsel moderation in requests of the gods, ask of Zeus that he protect them at least from evil marriages, and assert that though suffering is the lot of mankind they will be content if it is not their sole lot.

> **COMMENT:** The division of the Chorus has caused problems for editors. Some merely divide the fifty Danaids into two equal groups; others add a new, second Chorus of Maidservants. Both methods are structurally sound, though, at the time this play was written, a second chorus would have been a distinct innovation. It would not have been such a striking one by the time the play was probably produced, however. Zeus is depicted as being inscru-

table. Nonetheless, it is necessary to put one's faith in the ultimate goodness of all the gods (Artemis and Aphrodite are specifically mentioned), especially Zeus. The indefiniteness of the ending of *The Suppliant Maidens* obviously looks forward to the second and third lost plays of the trilogy for completion and clarification. The basic story is told in the Legend section of this chapter, but the absence of Aeschylus' treatment of the rest of the story is what has given rise to the different interpretations of the trilogy as a whole, and this play in particular.

THE PERSIANS

(472 B.C.)

BACKGROUND: *The Persians* was presented with three other plays of dissimilar subject matter: *Phineus, Glaucus Potnieus,* and *Prometheus the Fire-Bringer,* a satyr-play. The four plays won first prize. Pericles, later the most famous of all Athenian statesmen, was the choregus. This is the only one of the four dramas extant.

This play is unique in a number of ways. It is one of only three known Greek dramas of the fifth century, and the only surviving one, to deal with contemporary historical subjects. Because *The Persians* celebrates the Greek victory over the Persians in the naval battle at Salamis in 480 B.C., it would be expected to show the Persians in an unfavorable light. Such, however, is not the case. Aeschylus very daringly presents the Greeks' most determined and despotic enemies very sympathetically and with great nobility. Considering that the war between Persia and all of Greece was quite literally between slavery and freedom, and that Aeschylus himself and most of his audience fought at Salamis or Plataea (which the Greeks also won, in 479, and to which the Ghost of Darius refers in the play), the depiction of the Persians is unprecedented. It has also never been imitated since. Also unique, in this play glorifying a great Greek victory, is the absence of even the names of any Greek heroes. Many Persians are mentioned, some real, some made up by Aeschylus; the size of Xerxes' fleet at Salamis is exaggerated; the Persians invoke Greek gods; the Queen performs a Greek sacrifice at her husband's tomb; Darius is brought back from the past; and the action is set at Susa the capital of the Persian Empire, a place remote in space from Athens. All of these features help to give a tragic dignity to the drama. As in *The Suppliant Maidens,* the Chorus is the protagonist of this tragedy, and the Choral lyrics constitute about one-half of the extremely undramatic play.

THEMES: The major theme, naturally, is the glorification of the Greek, primarily the Athenian, victory over the Persians at Salamis. The corollary of this is the presentation of the working out of the Greek concept of hubris. Aeschylus says that too much success or prosperity will lead to excessive exaltation of self or nation (the hubris involved here), which in turn will inevitably lead to downfall, destruction, and ruin. For a further discussion of hubris, refer to the chapter on the development of fifth-century Athens.

HISTORICAL STORY: In 490 B.C. a Persian army led by Darius was defeated at Marathon, and in 481 the Persians, now under Xerxes, attempted to invade all of Greece. The Greeks lost the battle of Thermopylae, but won the battles of Salamis, in 480, and Plataea, in 479. When *The Persians* was produced, the victory it celebrates was only eight years in the past. For a fuller discussion of the Persian wars, see the chapter on the development of fifth-century Athens.

CHARACTERS:

CHORUS OF PERSIAN ELDERS Comprising the Persian Council of State.

ATOSSA Queen of Persia, widow of Darius, and mother of Xerxes.

HERALD Persian messenger.

GHOST OF DARIUS Former king of Persia and husband of Atossa, father of Xerxes.

XERXES King of Persia, son of Darius and Atossa.

ATTENDANTS Mute parts.

SETTING: The action takes place at Susa, the capital of Persia, shortly after the battle of Salamis in 480 B.C. In the background is the palace of Xerxes, which presumably also houses the Persian Council Chamber. In the center foreground is the tomb of Darius.

COMMENT: The palace is represented by the skene,

Darius' tomb by the altar of Dionysus in the center of the orchestra.

PROLOGUE AND PARODOS: The Chorus enters and the members identify themselves as the trusted servants appointed by King Xerxes to guard the realm in his absence. Because no news has been received from the Persian forces, the Chorus has presentiments of doom. Nonetheless, they give a listing of the many Persian heroes and leaders who accompanied Xerxes on his expedition, asserting that the army could only be all-conquering. Continuing, they describe what they hope has been the victorious advance of their army under the guidance of Xerxes and Ares, for the Persians are never defeated. Yet men are sometimes deceived by the gods, and thereby led to disaster. They pray for the safety and success of the army, saying that the Persian wives long for the safe return of their men. Seeing Atossa approaching, the Chorus kneels in obeisance to her.

COMMENT: Ares, son of Zeus and Hera, was the Greek god of war. This is the first instance in the play where Aeschylus has the Persians refer to a Greek rather than a Persian god. The Chorus' assertion that the Persians are always victorious is highly ironic, and no doubt was greatly appreciated by the Athenian audience. Historically, Darius himself had suffered a number of defeats, including two at the hands of the Greeks. The nobility of character with which Aeschylus has clothed the Persians is already evident in the opening words of the Chorus, as is his sympathy for the wives of soldiers, no matter who or where they might be.

FIRST EPISODE: Queen Atossa enters, splendidly adorned, in a horse-drawn chariot, accompanied by her retinue. She has come, she says, from her gold-bedecked palace, with premonitions of evil. Wealth the Persians have, but excessive wealth can lead to disaster. She is fearful for Xerxes, and has come to ask the Chorus for its counsel. She then tells of dreams she has had, in particular one that came to her the preceding night. Two women, one Persian, the other Greek, were yoked by her son, Xerxes, to a chariot. The Persian was obedient, but the Greek broke from her yoke and overturned Xerxes. With his dead father, Darius, looking on in anguish and pity, Xerxes rent his robes in grief. After Atossa arose that morning, she went to offer sacrifices to Apollo, but when she arrived at the altar she saw an eagle fleeing from a falcon which was clawing at its head. She says that should her son return victorious he will be greatly honored by the Persians, but even if he should be defeated he will still be king. The Chorus refuses to counsel in such a way that Atossa will be excessively fearful or confident, but rather advises that she offer prayers and sacrifices to the gods. Also, she should pray to her husband's spirit to aid her son. She will do so, she says, when she returns.

Meanwhile, she inquires the location of Athens. The Chorus tells of the large number of Greeks, their prowess at arms, and their wealth, all enough to deal the Persian host a grievous defeat. Suddenly a Herald enters, announcing the total defeat of the Persian army and navy at the battle of Salamis. An eyewitness of the battle, he describes the results of it in detail: lifeless, rotting corpses on the shore and fields, the ships sunk or scattered on the sea. Xerxes, he says, still lives, but he then enumerates some seventeen to twenty (depending upon the translation) Persian leaders who fell. He goes on to depict vividly the battle and its aftermath: the destruction of the Persian fleet in the Bay of Salamis; the flight of the survivors to the shore, where they were trapped and slaughtered; the order for the Persians to retreat, issued by Xerxes, who was watching the battle from a hill, seated on a golden throne after rending his cloak; and the final decimation of the army by drowning, starvation, and thirst as it attempted to get home. Even this does not reveal all of the horrors of the defeat, he says, a defeat engineered by the gods and inflicted by the ability and indomitableness of the Greeks. How else explain a victory by a force outnumbered, as the Greeks were, by a thousand ships to three hundred? The Herald departs, and Atossa mournfully says that she will now offer her prayers to the gods and Darius; no longer for victory, for the omens presented in her dreams have now been fulfilled, but for a better future.

COMMENT: Aeschylus, at the beginning of this Episode, presents one of many contrasts between the pomp of the Persians (Orientals and barbarians) and the simplicity of the Greeks. For a further discussion of Greek clothing, refer to the chapter on the development of the Greek theatre. Atossa's reference to the excessive wealth and luxury of the Persians is a concrete indication by the Per-

sian Queen herself of the hubris of the Persians. She invokes Apollo, another Greek rather than Persian god, in
his attribute as protector of travelers, namely, Xerxes and
the Persian army. Atossa's dream, of course, shows the
Greeks striving to break the yoke of Persian tyranny and
despotism, and succeeding; the falcon, a lesser bird than
the eagle, pursuing the eagle, portrays symbolically the
defeat and destruction of the Persian army at the hands of
a smaller force. It is significant that Atossa, after being
advised by the Chorus to offer prayers and sacrifices for
the army, postpones doing so until later. It is true that
even if offered immediately they would not have helped,
but the point Aeschylus is making is that prayers and sacrifices to the gods should be made when they are needed,
not later at one's convenience.

There is a certain amount of irony in the Queen's request
for information about Athens. It is true it is far distant
from Susa, but it is also true that as Queen she ought to
have known something about the city her son set out to
conquer. Of course, the question also enables Aeschylus to
have the Chorus say a number of flattering things about
his city. The Herald's description of the battle is the most
famous passage in the play. It is also the first surviving
long messenger's speech in literature, and is considered by
many to be the best. The enumeration by the Herald of
the degree to which the Greeks were outnumbered is a
deliberate exaggeration by Aeschylus to give added glory
to the Greeks, particularly the Athenian navy. The Greeks
were significantly outnumbered, but not as greatly as this.
It is also to be noted that the Herald, in describing the
Persian defeat, spends a good deal of time and breath
praising the Greeks, another method used by Aeschylus to
enable him to give patriotic praise to Athens.

FIRST STASIMON: The Chorus laments the Persian defeat,
acknowledging that it was brought about by Zeus to punish the
Persians for their pride. Many are the bereaved of Persia:
wives who are now widows; mothers and fathers who are without sons; and they, the elders of the land, who are now without
the flower of Persian manhood. Xerxes, in his vanity, led his
army in his ships, and the ships are now at the bottom of the
sea. Woe that he was not such a one as Darius, who was so

long and often victorious, and was adored by his people. The
authority of Persia has been destroyed, and Xerxes himself has
lost his regal power, for those whom the Persians held in sway
are now asserting their independence and freedom.

COMMENT: Darius was not as successful or well-beloved
as the Chorus asserts, but throughout the play Aeschylus
contrasts him with Xerxes, whom he portrays as the hated
(by the Greeks) and defeated ruler of Persia. The Greeks,
particularly the Athenians, are the freedom-loving people
the Chorus describes as revolting against the Persians.

SECOND EPISODE: Queen Atossa returns on foot, and more
simply dressed than she was earlier, asserting that humility is
better than vanity. She has come, she says, to offer libations to
Darius, and she asks the Chorus, also, to implore his spirit to
come and help them. The Chorus does so, and invokes Hermes
to lead Darius to them. While they sing their ode, Atossa performs her ritual by the tomb. When she and the Chorus have
finished, the Ghost of Darius rises from the tomb, wearing his
royal robes and crown. He asks what calamity has befallen
Persia that he has been called from the depths. On being informed of the destruction of the Persian host led by Xerxes,
Darius asks how it came about, and Atossa recounts the story
told by the Herald. Darius exclaims that the prophecy that
Zeus would punish Xerxes for his rashness has come to pass;
Xerxes, who tried in his youth to dam the Hellespont. Atossa
asserts that their son acted as he did because wicked men gave
him evil counsel; they complained that his father had made
conquests through war, while he merely imitated those victories
at sports.

Darius then recounts the history of Persia, telling how the nation grew in size and power through successive kings from Me-
dus to himself. Now the empire has been destroyed by his im-
petuous and vainglorious son, who is as young in age as in
sense. He advises that the Persians war no more with Greece,
lest they be utterly destroyed. As it is, few of the survivors of
the recent defeat will ever reach home alive, for they went in
pride and arrogance, destroyed temples of the gods, and were
bound to be punished. Indeed, the punishment and woe of the
Persians is not yet at an end, for another disaster awaits them
at Plataea. All this is the result of excessive pride and inso-

lence. He calls upon the Greeks, particularly the Athenians, not to make the same mistake, to be moderate in the exercise of their present good fortune, for Zeus punishes the insolent. After telling Atossa to go into the palace to get sumptuous robes for her son, who will shortly be returning, and who in his grief at the Persian defeat tore his clothes, Darius descends into the tomb. Atossa then leaves to carry out Darius' instructions.

> **COMMENT:** Aeschylus presents two major contrasts in this Episode. Earlier Queen Atossa entered in a chariot and wearing opulent robes. Then she was a proud queen looking for victory over the Greeks. Here she appears in humbler dress and on foot, for now she is a suppliant hoping to salvage whatever can be salvaged from the Persian defeat. Thus there is a contrast between vanity and humility. Here the Ghost of Darius appears in splendid royal robes and a crown, but his son Xerxes has been described as having torn his robes in grief and despair, and later he will appear in his dishevelment. There is a contrast between the successful and victorious king, and the unsuccessful and defeated one.
>
> Atossa performs her ritual in the Greek manner, another instance of Greek worship rather than Persian worship. Also, of course, the Chorus calls upon Hermes, a Greek god, who, in his attribute of messenger of the gods, had the responsibility of leading the spirits of the dead to the underworld. Here he is asked to reverse the procedure.
>
> This Episode contains the first instance of the appearance of a ghost in extant drama. It should be noted that he has only a limited amount of time to spend out of the underworld, and that his knowledge is the reverse of that of the living: he does not know anything about the present disaster at Salamis, but he is able to foretell the future defeat at Plataea. The Ghost's warning to the Persians to make no further war with the unconquerable Greeks is another example of Aeschylus' patriotic fervor.

SECOND STASIMON: The Chorus sings praises of Darius, mighty king, and the days when he expanded Persian power and glory, and brought wealth and dominance to the country. The army is no longer victorious, and Persia has been humbled.

COMMENT: This is a continuation of the contrast between the reign of Darius and that of Xerxes, and the concept that the gods, particularly Zeus, punish the sin of hubris.

EXODOS: Xerxes enters, alone, and with his robes torn. He laments the fate that has befallen him through the will of the gods. He and the Chorus grieve over the disaster that has come upon Persia, as he tells of the defeat at Salamis, the deaths of the Persian leaders, the destruction of the army, and how he rent his robes in woe at the sight of all these things. He calls upon the members of the Chorus to similarly rend their robes, tear their hair, and weep as they bewail the fate that has befallen Persia. After doing so, the Chorus accompanies Xerxes to his palace.

COMMENT: The contrast between Darius and Xerxes is now complete, and Xerxes again emphasizes that hubris inevitably leads to downfall.

SEVEN AGAINST THEBES

(467 B.C.)

BACKGROUND: Aeschylus won first prize for his Theban tetralogy, which included *Laius, Oedipus, Seven Against Thebes*, and *The Sphinx*, a satyr-play. Of these, only *Seven Against Thebes* has survived. The play is rather static, simple in structure, and bombastic in many places.

THEMES: The theme that was probably basic to the whole trilogy, of which this play was the concluding one, no doubt was that the sins of the fathers are visited upon the sons, for the trilogy presented the downfall of Laius and his descendants. The theme and story, therefore, parallel those of the *Oresteia*. The second part of *Seven Against Thebes* is chiefly concerned with the fate of the House of Laius, and since this part concludes the entire trilogy it lends considerable weight to the conclusion that the above-mentioned is the overall theme. However, the first part of the play concerns the fate of Thebes and the intense personal feuds of the Argive leaders and their great arrogance. Consequently, Aeschylus is also saying that an attack on one's native city cannot be justified and will lead to doom, and that the sin of hubris, in this case arrogance, will inevitably be punished. That Aeschylus belonged to the generation which had witnessed the expulsion of the tyrant Hippias from Athens and his subsequent return as a leader of an invading Persian army which was defeated at Marathon, and the ostracism and exile of Themistocles, savior of Athens and Greece at the battle of Salamis, from Athens and his subsequent going-over to the Persians, lends considerable weight to the former of these secondary themes. The punishment of the sin of hubris was a major or secondary theme in virtually all Greek tragedies.

LEGEND: Laius, King of Thebes, and his wife Jocasta were childless for some time. To find out why, Laius consulted the

54

oracle at Delphi. On being told his childlessness was a blessing in disguise, because any child born of Jocasta would eventually kill him, he returned home and, without saying why, put his wife away. She, vexed, got him drunk and he lay with her. When her child was born Laius seized him, pierced his feet, tied them together, and had him exposed on Mount Cithaeron. The baby was found by a shepherd, who named him Oedipus, "he of the swollen feet," and brought him to Corinth, where King Polybus and his wife Periboea raised him as their son. Jeered at by other youths because he bore no resemblance to his supposed parents, Oedipus went to Delphi to ask the oracle what his future was to be. He was informed that he would kill his father and marry his mother.

Not wishing to bring any harm to Polybus and Periboea, Oedipus exiled himself, but in a narrow pass he encountered a chariot in which were Laius and Polyphontes, his charioteer, who were themselves on their way to Delphi. After disputing the right of way, Oedipus, in anger, killed both riders, and proceeded toward Thebes. He came upon the Sphinx, answered her riddle, thus causing her to fling herself to her death, and was acclaimed by the Thebans, who made him king and gave him their newly widowed queen, Jocasta, as his wife. By Jocasta, Oedipus had four children: twin sons, Eteocles and Polyneices; and two daughters, Antigone and Ismene. When a plague, said by the blind seer Teiresias to have been caused by the fact that the murderer of Laius had never been punished, descended on Thebes, Oedipus, in the course of trying to learn the identity of the criminal, discovered that he himself had done the deed. Jocasta thereupon hanged herself. Oedipus put his eyes out, and exiled himself from Thebes, appointing his sons to rule the kingdom in alternate years. Before leaving, however, Eteocles and Polyneices insulted him, whereupon he cursed them both. After wandering for many years, Oedipus finally died at Colonus.

Eteocles, the first of the brothers to rule Thebes, refused to give up the throne at the end of the year, and banished Polyneices from the city. Polyneices went to Argos, where he married Aegeia, one of the daughters of King Adrastus, and implored Adrastus for help in regaining his kingdom. Adrastus and four other Argive chieftains, Capaneus, Hippomedon, Amphiaraus, and Parthenopaeus, together with Polyneices and Tydeus of Calydon, went with an expedition to besiege Thebes. The Thebans were victorious in the war, and all of the attacking champions were killed with the exception of Adrastus. Eteocles and Polyneices killed each other in the battle outside the city, thereby fulfilling their father's curse, and Creon, their uncle, became king. He decreed that none of the dead champions, including Polyneices, were to be buried, and when Antigone buried her brother's body anyway, he had her killed. Haemon, Creon's son, who was to have married Antigone, thereupon killed himself. The sons of the champions who had fallen before Thebes, who were known as the Epigoni, "those who were born afterwards," swore vengeance on Thebes, and eventually conquered, sacked, and razed the city.

CHARACTERS:

ETEOCLES   Son of Oedipus, brother of Polyneices, and present King of Thebes.

ANTIGONE ⎫
            ⎬   Sisters of Eteocles.
ISMENE   ⎭

MESSENGER   A scout, or spy, of the Theban army.

HERALD

CHORUS OF THEBAN WOMEN

SIX CHAMPIONS ⎫
                ⎪
CITIZENS OF THEBES ⎬   Mute parts.
                ⎪
ATTENDANTS ⎭

SETTING: The action takes place inside the city of Thebes. There are a number of statues of Greek gods and a central altar. A crowd of Thebans is on stage as Eteocles enters.

   COMMENT: The altar is represented by the altar of Dionysus at the center of the orchestra.

PROLOGUE: Eteocles addresses the Thebans, citizens of

Cadmus, telling them that he does not know how the war will go, for them or against them, and calls upon Zeus to defend him and the city. He exhorts all to defend their country, the shrines of their gods, and the very life-giving soil of Thebes itself against the invaders. A seer has told him that the enemy army is shortly to mount its strongest attack; therefore, to the battlements, the towers, and the bulwarks, and stand firm against the foreigners. Do not fear the attackers, he says, for the gods will defend us, and in addition he has sent scouts and spies into the besieging army who will shortly report its dispositions to him. A Messenger, one of the scouts, enters to give his report. He has seen, he says, seven of the enemy's mighty champions swear an oath to raze the city or die in the attempt. He left them casting lots to see which of the city's seven gates each would attack with his men. He urges Eteocles to see to the defense of the gates, and leaves to obtain further information. Eteocles calls upon Zeus, the gods of Thebes, and his father's curse not to bring about the destruction of the city, and leaves with his attendants and most of the crowd.

COMMENT: Eteocles calls the Thebans "citizens of Cadmus," and nowhere in the play are the words "Thebes" or "Thebans" used. Cadmus was the ancient name of Thebes, so called because it had been founded by Cadmus, son of Agenor, King of Tyre. Thebes had become an ally of Persia during the invasion which had recently ended at Salamis and Plataea, and was consequently in disgrace with the rest of the Greeks. The use of the terms "Cadmus" and "Cadmeans" by Aeschylus no doubt reflects his patriotic fervor and his desire not to offend the feelings of the Athenians. Eteocles invokes Zeus, the supreme god of the Greeks, in his attributes of protector of kings and the social order. Because they insulted him and supported those who wished to expel him from Thebes, Oedipus laid a curse upon Eteocles and Polyneices: they would slay each other fighting over the city.

PARODOS: Appearing terror-stricken, the Chorus of Theban Women enters. Shouts and cries from the city's walls are heard as the Chorus chants its fears of the attackers and its pleas to the gods to protect Thebes. Fearful anticipation is stronger than arms, they say, as they hear the sounds of spears clashing on shields, war-chariots racing round the city's walls, and stones showering on the battlements. Throughout they implore the gods to defend them.

COMMENT: The psychology presented here is striking. It has become almost a commonplace saying that fear is the mother of defeat. Eteocles, when he reappears in the following Episode, rebukes the Chorus much as Shakespeare, who wrote that fear makes traitors of us all, might have.

FIRST EPISODE: Eteocles re-enters with his retinue and chides the Chorus for their cowardly fears, their blind faith in the gods, and their continual howling in the city's streets which is unnerving the people. He orders them to obey him, for women have no business interfering in the activities of men, and if they do not he will decree their deaths. The Chorus attempts to justify itself, and Eteocles repeats that he wants obedient silence from them; it is a time for bravery and courage, not wailing in the streets. He will not tolerate their making cowards of his troops, especially since it is his responsibility to encourage the army and bolster its morale. If they wish to pray, they should do it calmly and quietly, as he is about to do. He then prays to the Theban gods to deliver the city, and swears that if they do so the Thebans will offer them enormous sacrifices. He, himself, will adorn their altars with spoils taken from the invaders. He then leaves with his retinue to choose six other champions, himself being the seventh, to defend the city's gates.

COMMENT: This Episode and the preceding Parodos are magnificent depictions of the fears, tensions, and panic that can so easily possess the inhabitants of a besieged city. Aeschylus is saying that they are best controlled through the exercising of calm and firm leadership.

FIRST STASIMON: The Chorus reverts to its panicky state, half-heartedly calling upon the gods for protection, but vividly visualizing the downfall of Thebes. The invaders will destroy, pillage, rape, slaughter the men, and carry the women off to become slaves.

COMMENT: This scene is also of great psychological interest, for Aeschylus is saying that when the firm leadership is removed (Eteocles has left the stage), the followers will revert to their fearful, cowardly, and defeatist state of mind.

SECOND EPISODE: The Messenger enters from one side of the stage, and Eteocles from the other. Eteocles has with him six Theban champions. The Messenger tells Eteocles which Argive champion is at each Theban gate, and describes his armament, dwelling with particular detail on his shield. As each is described, Eteocles dispatches a Theban hero to match him. He sends Melanippus to oppose Tydeus; Polyphontes to match Capaneus; Megareus to fight Eteoclus; Hyperbius to resist Hippomedon; Actor to withstand Parthenopaeus; and Lasthenes to confront Amphiaraus the seer, who, says the Messenger, has bitterly denounced Tydeus as a murderer and Polyneices as one who has brought dishonor on himself and the Argives through his war on his native city and gods, and then predicted his own death during the attack. All of the Theban champions have been dispatched, and the Messenger now announces that Polyneices himself, Eteocles' brother, will assault the seventh gate. Polyneices, relates the Messenger, has declared his desire to fight Eteocles to the death, or if Eteocles survives the conquest of Thebes, to banish him. Eteocles, recalling his father's curse, nonetheless declares that he will himself confront his brother at the seventh gate. The Chorus attempts to dissuade him, referring also to Oedipus' curse, saying that there are others who can fight Polyneices. Eteocles is adamant, asserting that he will not dishonor himself by not fighting with his brother, and, gloomily predicting his own death, he goes out to meet it.

COMMENT: This Episode, which comes precisely in the middle of the play (there are 368 lines before and 365 after it) and occupies one-third of it (350 lines), is generally considered to be a flaw, for the enumeration of the Argive and Theban heroes is essentially epic in nature rather than dramatic. Even so, the scene is well constructed, for it rises to a climax with Amphiaraus' condemnation of his own cause, and it concludes with Eteocles as the only one left to be the champion who will face his brother. And his honor will not allow him to sidestep his responsibility, even though he clearly foresees that he will die at his brother's hands.

Melanippus was the son of Astacus. During the battle he

killed Tydeus, but was himself slain by Amphiaraus. Tydeus was the son of King Oeneus of Calydon. He had a brother named Melanippus, and it was prophesied that Melanippus would kill him. Tydeus killed his brother when hunting one day, which is why Amphiaraus calls him a murderer. As indicated above, he was killed by the Theban Melanippus. Virtually nothing is known about Polyphontes. Capaneus was the son of Hipponous. While attempting to scale the walls of Thebes he foolishly boasted that not even lightning could frighten him, and Zeus struck him dead with one of his thunderbolts. Megareus, King of Boetia, a descendant of the Sparti, the armed men who sprang from the dragon's teeth sown by Cadmus, founder of the city which later became Thebes, sacrificed his life in the battle after Tiresias, the blind seer, had foretold that Thebes would be victorious if one of the Sparti voluntarily gave his life. Eteoclus, son of Iphis, is listed here by Aeschylus as one of the seven Argive champions in place of Adrastus, who was the military leader of the expedition. Nothing further is known about him. Nothing at all is known about Hyperbius, son of Oenops. Hippomedon was an Argive king about whom there is no further information. Virtually nothing definite is known about Actor. Parthenopaeus, son of Meleager and Atalanta, was an Arcadian ally of Adrastus. He was killed by a rock while storming the walls of the city. There is no information concerning Lasthenes. Amphiaraus, son of Oecles and Hypermnestra, the only one of the Danaids who refused to kill her husband (who at the time was Lynceus), was the brother-in-law of Adrastus. A seer, he at first refused to join the expedition since he foresaw that all of the Argive heroes, including himself and with the sole exception of Adrastus, would be killed. His wife, Eriphyle, Adrastus' sister, forced him to take part in the war. As he was about to be speared by a Theban, Zeus split the earth open with a thunderbolt and he was swallowed up to reign, alive, among the dead.

SECOND STASIMON: The Chorus mournfully recalls Oedipus' curse upon his sons, and dreads that they will kill each other in shame and sin. They recount the history of the House of Laius, which itself has borne a continuing curse ever since Laius allowed himself to be seduced by his wife after he had heard the oracle's warning. Woe follows upon woe in an unending chain.

COMMENT: For the history of the House of Laius, refer to the Legend section of this chapter.

THIRD EPISODE: The Messenger re-enters and proclaims the defeat of the Argives, the deaths of the six Argive champions, and the fulfillment of Oedipus' curse: Eteocles and Polyneices have slain each other in front of the seventh gate.

COMMENT: Thus, says Aeschylus, is evil bound up with good: the city has been saved, but the curse of Oedipus has been realized.

THIRD STASIMON: The Chorus cannot decide whether to rejoice over the deliverance of Thebes or lament over the deaths of Eteocles and Polyneices, dead as the result of their father's curse, and the even older curse placed on the House of Laius. The bodies of the two princes are carried in, escorted by their sisters, Antigone and Ismene, and a procession of mourners. The Chorus and the two sisters alternate in chanting a dirge over the bodies, again detailing the sorrows of the House of Laius.

COMMENT: Aeschylus again presents the concept that evil and sin are self-perpetuating, and that a family curse is virtually impossible to remove.

EXODOS: The Chorus, Antigone, and Ismene continue their dirge, and a Herald enters to declare that the Theban council has decreed that Eteocles is to be given an honorable burial, due to one who died defending his city bravely and patriotically, but that Polyneices, a traitor who attacked his city, is to be left, unburied, as food for birds and dogs. Antigone declares that she will defy the council and bury her brother's body, irrespective of the consequences to herself. She bears more allegiance to their mutual blood than to Thebes. The Herald warns her against violating the decree of the council, but she remains adamant. The Chorus mourns the destruction of Oedipus' family, and voices fears that further calamities will result from Antigone's decision. The chorus divides itself into two groups, one asserting support of her, the other of the decision of the council.

> **COMMENT:**   Most authorities consider this final scene to be spurious, for if it were genuine, Antigone's decision would leave the action of the play unfinished. But the play is the concluding one of a trilogy, and it is most unlikely that Aeschylus would leave the ending hanging like this. Interestingly enough, however, Antigone's determination to bury her brother's body because a blood tie claims a higher allegiance than does loyalty to the state creates an ethical problem which is dealt with in detail in Sophocle's tragedy *Antigone* and Euripides' lost drama of the same name.

PROMETHEUS BOUND

(Date Unknown)

BACKGROUND: Little is definitely known about the production of *Prometheus Bound*, though it seems likely that it was the first play of a trilogy, the other two of which were probably *Prometheus Unbound* and *Prometheus the Fire-Bringer*. It is known that a satyr-play, *Prometheus (the Fire-Lighter)*, was one of the plays produced with *The Persians* in 472 B.C. The staging of this play undoubtedly caused great difficulty, for action of any kind is absolutely impossible for Prometheus since he is chained to a cliff. Consequently, the drama is quite static, though there is considerable psychological conflict. The production was evidently extremely spectacular since Might, Violence, and Hephaestus probably affixed a wooden figure, larger than life-size, to the cliff with chains and a wedge hammered through the chest at the beginning of the drama. The cliff itself seems to have been of considerable height, perhaps higher than the skene, which had an elevation of ten to twelve feet. The importance of the chorus is reduced considerably, as is its size. It probably numbered only twelve members, and its common function of introducing characters is taken from it, no doubt due to Prometheus' continual presence and presumed omniscience. As is also true of the *Agamemnon*, no secondary character appears more than once during the play.

THEMES: Because the rest of the trilogy has been lost, any attempt to interpret *Prometheus Bound* is risky. The basic problem presented would appear to be: What is the true and ultimate nature of the divine power and authority which underlies and controls the universe? Furthermore, if that power is benevolent, why is there evil and suffering in the world? A corollary of this would be the basic conflict between brute force or violence and intelligence or justice. Certainly there is a presentation of Zeus as a new and therefore tyrannical ruler of the universe, and the suggestion that he became more beneficent as time went on. Therefore, the overall theme of the whole trilogy

63

might well have involved his recognition and adoption of wisdom and justice.

LEGEND: After Mother Earth (Gaea) arose from Chaos, she gave birth to Uranus, who became the supreme god. He and Gaea had a number of children, including the twelve Titans. One of them, Cronus, led the rest in a revolt against their father, whom they succeeded in overthrowing. Cronus thereupon became the chief god. Iapetus, another of the Titans, became the father of several gods, including Atlas, Epimetheus, and Prometheus, who, while not members of the original group of Titans, were nonetheless called by that name. Cronus himself fathered Zeus, Poseidon, Hades, Hera, Demeter, and Hestia, none of whom were ever called Titans. Zeus decided to lead his brothers and sisters in a revolt against Cronus and the other Titans, including those of the second generation. Prometheus was told by his mother that Cronus could never be successful if he used force alone; only cunning would succeed against the rebels. He told Cronus this, and when Cronus ignored his advice Prometheus went over to Zeus' side, which was victorious. Zeus then became the supreme god. Shortly afterward Zeus decided to destroy mankind, which had become base and contemptuous of the gods. Prometheus, who was believed to have created mankind out of clay and water, opposed him. Since Prometheus had already angered Zeus by taking fire from Mount Olympus, the home of the gods, and giving it to man, Zeus had no compunctions about punishing him. He chained him to a cliff in the Caucasus, where a vulture tore at his liver all day long. During the night the liver grew whole again so the next day the vulture could resume his feasting. Prometheus endured this punishment for many generations, being visited by many people, including Io, in the meantime, before he was at last freed by Heracles.

CHARACTERS:

MIGHT   Servant of Zeus.

VIOLENCE   Another servant of Zeus. Mute part.

HEPHAESTUS   Son of Zeus and Hera, god of fire and the blacksmith's art. As the god of handicrafts he did the metalworking for Zeus and the other gods.

PROMETHEUS A Titan son of Iapetus. He went over to Zeus' side when Zeus revolted against Cronus and the other Titans.

OCEANUS Titan son of Uranus and Gaea who was god of the sea prior to Poseidon.

IO One of the mortal women with whom Zeus fell in love. Hera, Zeus' wife, in her jealousy changed her into a white cow and forced her to wander throughout the world while being constantly stung by a gadfly.

HERMES Son of Zeus and Maia. He was the god of dexterity and cunning, but was chiefly used by Zeus and the other gods as their messenger.

CHORUS OF DAUGHTERS OF OCEANUS

SETTING: The drama is set on a rocky and desolate crag in the Caucasus in Scythia, a region in southeastern Europe and Asia. Its precise boundaries have not been determined, but it was presumably between the Black Sea and the Caspian Sea in the southwestern part of what is now the Soviet Union.

PROLOGUE: Might and Violence enter, carrying Prometheus as a prisoner. Hephaestus accompanies them. Might announces that they have come to Scythia, the desolate limit of the world. He tells Hephaestus that he must now follow the Father's command to chain Prometheus to the crag as punishment for giving Hephaestus' fire to men. Prometheus must learn to acknowledge the sovereignty of Zeus and stop loving mankind so much. Hephaestus says he is unwilling to chain another god, who is also a relation, but he is too afraid of Zeus to disobey his order. The result of Prometheus' love for men will be his isolation from men; chained to this rock, he will be scorched by the sun all day, and frozen by the cold all night, in never-ending torment, for there is no man born who can help him. Zeus' will is harsh and adamant, as is true of every ruler whose power has been newly acquired. As Might relentlessly directs Hephaestus to do what he is there to do, Hephaestus, reluctantly obeying, emphasizes to Prometheus that he is following Zeus' will and not his own. Might urges Hephaestus to strike the hammer harder, bind the chain tighter, and finally to drive a

wedge through Prometheus' chest; sympathy for an enemy of
Zeus ill becomes a god and should be controlled, lest it result
in new enmity from the Father. When the shackling is com-
pleted, Hephaestus departs, and Might taunts Prometheus for
being called Forethought, and asks contemptuously if he thinks
the mortals he cared for so much can or will help him now.
Might then leaves, and Prometheus, left alone, calls upon all of
Nature to witness what he, a god, must endure at the hands of
other gods. He laments his present sorrow and his sorrow to
come, and asks rhetorically if there will ever be an end to it.
And all this because he cared for and aided mankind. Suddenly
he senses the presence of other beings.

> COMMENT: As the setting indicates and Might empha-
> sizes, Prometheus is to be isolated from both gods and
> men. The Caucasus was relatively unknown to the Greeks,
> at the extreme outer limit of their world. Might and Vio-
> lence are absolute servants and manifestations of Zeus, as
> indeed is indicated by both Hephaestus and Might himself.
> Consequently Might (Violence has no lines) is only inter-
> ested in having Prometheus' punishment carried out; he
> has no compassion for him at all. Characters like Might
> and Violence are known as personified abstractions, and
> their words and actions are necessarily consistent with the
> attributes of the abstract ideas they represent. Therefore,
> they are less complicated and less able to show develop-
> ment than characters with more realistic personalities. In
> context, however, they serve a definite function, and serve
> it well. Zeus, of course, was known as the Father of gods
> and men.
>
> Zeus and Prometheus were both sons of Titans, and are
> consequently first cousins. Hephaestus, Zeus' son, is there-
> fore Prometheus' first cousin, once removed. His reluc-
> tance to punish his cousin-god is interesting because Zeus
> has no such compunctions. Might refers to Prometheus'
> theft of Hephaestus' fire (it was his because he was the
> god of fire) in an unsuccessful attempt to lessen Hephaes-
> tus' sympathy for Prometheus. It is obvious at this point
> that neither Zeus nor his representatives, Might and Vio-
> lence, have any compassion at all, but as Hephaestus says,
> this is to be expected of new rulers.
>
> Both Hephaestus and Might are unknowingly ironic when

they say that there is no man who will help Prometheus as he helped mankind, for there is no such man alive at the time. But Prometheus has foreknowledge (which is why he is called Forethought), as he indicates in his rhetorical question, and states specifically, later in the play, that Heracles, a later son of Zeus, will come generations later to release him.

PARODOS: The Chorus of Oceanids enters in a winged chariot, saying that they heard the sound of hammering all the way down in their cavernous home beneath the sea. They have come to learn the cause of the noise. On being told by Prometheus that he is being punished, they say that Zeus has cast aside the old laws and made up new ones to suit himself. Prometheus exclaims that he would rather Zeus had hurled him into the depths of Tartarus, where at least neither gods nor his enemies could come to exult over his torment. The Oceanids find it impossible to believe that any of the gods except Zeus would find delight in Prometheus' degradation and torture, and Zeus will be the same until he becomes satiated or is overthrown. Prometheus declares that the day will indeed come when Zeus will be threatened with dethronement, and he will then need Prometheus to thwart the plot. But, swears Prometheus, he will give neither information nor aid until Zeus has freed and recompensed him. The Oceanids commiserate with Prometheus for the anguish his determined stand will surely bring him, and he again alludes to the secret he alone knows which will ultimately soften Zeus' hard heart.

COMMENT: The Oceanids and their chariot appear by way of the mechane, which is a good indication of the relative smallness of the Chorus as well as the strength of the mechane. For a further discussion of the mechane, see the chapter on the Greek theatre.

Tartarus, which was below Hades, was the most terrible part of the underworld. It was a bottomless pit where Zeus shut up various monsters, the Titans, and others with whom he became enraged.

Prometheus' secret concerned Thetis, a sea goddess, of whom Zeus was enamoured. Prometheus, through his foreknowledge, knew that if Thetis had a son he was fated to be more powerful than his father; therefore, if Zeus were the father he would be overthrown. When Zeus finally learned of this from Prometheus, he arranged for Thetis to be married to Peleus, a mortal. The son turned out to be Achilles, who was indeed more powerful than his father.

Aeschylus presents Zeus as a symbol of an outside force which desires to exercise absolute tyranny over intellect and spirit, represented by Prometheus. But the latter must, of necessity, be free from outside domination if they are to function properly and freely, though this does not mean that intellect should be allowed to operate with license; it needs some kind of direction. This is why many feel that the trilogy as a whole ended with some kind of compromise between Zeus and Prometheus, with Zeus adopting wisdom and Prometheus accepting Zeus' leadership and direction. Interestingly enough, while Zeus is condemned by Prometheus and the Chorus for his obstinate tyranny, Prometheus is just as obstinate in asserting his independence, not only of mind, but also of action (in giving fire to mankind). Both are equally unyielding, but Prometheus, says Aeschylus, is being punished unjustly and is therefore right in being stubborn. Whether or not the other gods are really sympathetic to him is debatable, for the Oceanids' remarks may simply be hyperbole. In any case, Prometheus is certainly receiving a poor reward for the help he has already given Zeus in the past.

FIRST EPISODE: The Chorus asks Prometheus to tell them what he did to incur Zeus' wrath, and he recounts the story of the revolt of Zeus and the gods of his generation against Cronus and the other Titans. When Cronus refused Prometheus' advice to use cunning, Prometheus joined Zeus' side and aided in his victory. After Zeus had handed out rewards to those who had helped him, he decided to destroy mankind; Prometheus alone opposed him. Since to the Oceanids the punishment Zeus has inflicted seems out of proportion to Prometheus' crime, they ask him if he, perhaps, did more than this. His answer is yes, he gave man blind hopes so that he would be able to forget his inevitable doom, death, and fire so that he would be able to learn many skills. It is for *these* things that Zeus is punishing him, declares Prometheus, and he did them willingly,

even though he knew what the result would be. He bids the
Oceanids to step out of their chariot so that he can tell them
what is yet to come. They do so, and suddenly Oceanus arrives, riding a hippocampus, and asks Prometheus how he can
help him. Prometheus is astonished that Oceanus had the courage to leave the safety of his ocean home, and somewhat sar-
castically asks if he came simply to observe his torment.
Oceanus rather fussily advises Prometheus to submit to the new
tyrant, cease his defiance, curb his tongue, and consider his
own well-being, and he himself will speak to Zeus on his behalf. Prometheus replies that Oceanus would do well to take his
own advice, because his intercession with Zeus would do no
good and might even bring harm to Oceanus, for Zeus has
vented his wrath on others, too. By way of illustration, Prometheus recalls the fates of his brother Atlas, condemned to support the pillar of earth and heaven on his shoulders, and Typho, buried under Mount Aetna. Oceanus, seeing Prometheus'
plight as a more pertinent example, takes his advice and leaves
for his home.

COMMENT: For a more detailed history of Prometheus'
deeds, see the Legend section to this play. That Prometheus gave his gifts to mankind willingly, even though he
had foreknowledge of the outcome, is one of the cruxes of
the drama. Aeschylus is saying that knowledge or wisdom
must not cease to contest with brute force and violence,
no matter what the real or apparent danger might be. He
is also saying that wisdom brings compassion, and the
foregoing of help from Oceanus because of the possible
danger to him is an example of this.

Oceanus was a son of Uranus and Gaea. He was the original god of the sea and all waters. Later, of course, Poseidon, Zeus' brother and one of the new gods, became the
sea god. The hippocampus Oceanus arrives on was a sea
monster with the head and forequarters of a horse and the
tail of a fish, presumably a large-size sea horse. Oceanus
undoubtedly was lowered on the mechane, which is presumably why the Oceanids got off it.

Atlas was a son of Iapetus, and therefore Prometheus'
brother. He sided with Cronus against Zeus, and indeed
was the war-leader of the Titans. After the Titans were

defeated Zeus compelled him to carry the heavens, or the pillars on which they rested, on his shoulders. Typho, or Typhon, was a son of Tartarus and Gaea. He had a hundred fire-breathing heads, a hundred arms and legs in the form of snakes, and was of gigantic size. He attacked the gods and put all of them to flight except Zeus, who, even though wounded, finally overcame him with his thunderbolts and buried him under Mount Aetna in Sicily.

FIRST STASIMON: The Chorus laments the suffering of the two Titans, Prometheus and Atlas. All of Nature, they say, mourns for Prometheus.

>**COMMENT:** This, of course, recalls and constitutes an answer to Prometheus' invoking, in the Prologue, of all of Nature to witness his plight.

SECOND EPISODE: Prometheus speaks of all the gifts he gave to mankind: the use of the mind; the building of houses; the observation and use of the seasons; the knowledge of numbers and the alphabet; the writing of history; the domestication of animals; the construction and use of sailing ships; the use of medicine; the art of divination and the foretelling of the future; the proper way to make ritual offerings to the gods; and the use of metals. Before he gave these gifts, he says, mankind was in a sad and pitiable condition, but now they have been ennobled. The Oceanids declare that he did not exercise expediency when he helped mortals; he worried too much about them and not enough about himself. But perhaps one day he will again be free, and the equal of Zeus. Prometheus says that the Fates, to whom even Zeus must bow his will, have decreed that he will be freed, but that the time has not yet come, and he hints again at the secret which he must keep to himself, for it is his only weapon against Zeus.

>**COMMENT:** Greek mythology included what were referred to as the Five Ages of Man. In the first, or Golden Age, during which Cronus was in power, men were happy and did not need either to till the land or work. In the Silver Age Zeus came to power and introduced the four seasons of the year, thus making necessary the building of houses and labor. The Bronze Age followed, during which men learned to use metals. They also became insolent, to

each other and to the gods. Then came the Heroic Age, during which men improved somewhat because many of them were sons of gods by mortal mothers. Last came the Iron Age, which was made up of the unworthy descendants of the Heroic Age. Crime became rampant, men became utterly miserable, and labor became toil. All of the good qualities of man were cast aside and the evil ones came to the fore. At this point Zeus became so disgusted that he decided to destroy mankind and start again. This myth explained what the Greeks felt was the progressive degeneration of mankind. Aeschylus can easily be considered to be either telescoping this myth or reversing it, but in either case the myth was no doubt in the minds of his audience.

Zeus was the supreme god, and none of the other gods could stand against him. Nonetheless, even he was believed to be subject to what was variously called Fate or the Three Fates, the force which measured out and largely governed man's life.

SECOND STASIMON: The Oceanids voice the hope that they will never incur Zeus' wrath. They sympathize with Prometheus, but point out that he did, after all, bring his punishment on himself: he did not fear Zeus enough or bow to his will; in fact, he self-willedly contravened Zeus' wishes, and was too much of a friend to man. And why bother with man, a feeble creature subject to death who can do nothing to aid Prometheus in return? They conclude by comparing his present plight with a happer time: his wedding day.

COMMENT: The Chorus is saying, of course, that by his excessive love for man, Prometheus overstepped the boundary of moderation, and committed the sin of hubris.

THIRD EPISODE: Io enters, partly transformed into a heifer, and pursued by the ghost of Argus in the form of a gadfly. As Argus stings her, she dances in a frenzy. Distracted, she asks where she is and who is being tortured and why. Then she implores Zeus to tell her why he is allowing her to be tormented, and again asks Prometheus who he is and if he can tell her how much suffering she still has to undergo. He is about to reply when the Oceanids, who have been observing Io in wonderment, ask her to tell them why she is being punished. She says that when she was younger she had dreams in which voices told her that Zeus had fallen in love with her, and that she should go into the meadow to meet him. She finally became so upset that she told her father, Inachus, of the dreams, and he consulted the oracle at Delphi for advice. The oracle said that if he did not cast Io out of his house, Zeus would destroy his entire family with a thunderbolt. Inachus, albeit unwillingly, obeyed. Io was immediately transformed, beset by the gadfly. and watched over by Argus. Argus was subsequently killed, but she is still pursued by the gadfly and has been forced to wander from land to land. Finished with her story, she implores Prometheus to tell her, if he can, what the future holds for her. He reveals that she must endure many more wanderings, travel through many lands, and cross many waters, including the Bosporus which shall be named after her. He then turns to the Chorus to comment on Zeus, the tyrant of the gods, who brought this suffering on a mortal merely because he desired to lie with her. And even this is not all that Io will have to undergo. She asks if there will never be a way of overthrowing Zeus, and Prometheus again alludes to his secret, emphasizing that Zeus can save himself only by freeing him from his bonddage. And, indeed, it will be one of Io's descendants, thirteen generations hence, who will bring about his release. Prometheus then completes his prophecy of Io's rovings, saying that finally Zeus will touch her, thus transforming her to her mortal form, ending her torment, and causing her to give birth to Epaphus, from whose line will come the hero who will release him. The gadfly begins to sting Io again, and she dances off in a frenzy.

COMMENT: In contrast to the Chorus and Oceanus, who enter on the mechane and never descend to the orchestra, Io enters in the orchestra and never ascends the crag on which Prometheus is chained. This gives her adequate space for her frenzied dances. Further details of her story are used by Aeschylus in *The Suppliant Maidens*. Though it was through Zeus' love for Io that she was tormented, and of course Prometheus condemns Zeus for allowing it to take place, it was actually jealous Hera who transformed her and also set Argus, a hundred-eyed monster, as a guard over her. Zeus sent Hermes to rescue Io, and after lulling Argus to sleep by playing his flute, he cut off

the monster's head. Hera thereupon sent a gadfly to
sting Io and cause her to wander throughout the world.
Gadflies are actually large horseflies that make it a practice to sting cattle. The Bosporus was said by the Greeks
to have been named after Io because Bosporus means
cow's-ford. The "touching" of Io by Zeus is a reference to
the mystical relationship between the gods and man which
constitutes one of the themes of *The Suppliant Maidens*.
Details concerning Epaphus and his descendants are also
used by Aeschylus in *The Suppliant Maidens*, and further
information concerning them can be found in the Comments to that drama. The particular descendant referred
to by Prometheus is, of course, Heracles.

In this Episode, which is the longest section of the play, a
contrast is presented between Prometheus, who openly
defied Zeus and is being punished for his defiance, and Io,
who had the misfortune to arouse Zeus' lust and is being
tormented by Hera out of jealousy. But Zeus is allowing
her torment to take place, and, as Prometheus asserts, this
makes him doubly a tyrant: first, for permitting the torment, and second, because it is undeserved. Io is, therefore, an innocent victim of a monstrous tyranny, and by
extension Aeschylus is saying that tyranny in human government is just as monstrous, for it affects the guilty and
the innocent alike.

THIRD STASIMON: Giving point to Io's story, the Chorus
declares that it is better by far for equals to marry with equals.
They fervently desire to be spared the love of Zeus or any
other superior gods, but they concede that if Zeus were to desire them they would be unable to withstand him.

> **COMMENT:** Just as at the end of the preceding Episode
> the audience was given a lesson in politics, they are now
> being given a lesson in human relations. Love or marriage
> between people of unequal station or wealth can only lead
> to trouble; therefore, love and marriage between equals is
> best for everyone.

EXODOS: Prometheus, recalling the curse Cronus placed upon
Zeus when his son dethroned him, prophesys that it will inevitably come to pass, and Zeus will be overthrown, unless Pro-

metheus reveals the secret of Thetis to him. Doubtfully, the Chorus recommends that Prometheus curb his tongue lest Zeus inflict even more severe punishment on him. At this point Hermes enters, to be greeted contemptuously by Prometheus as Zeus' lackey. Hermes harangues Prometheus for his lack of respect for the other gods, and says that Father Zeus has overheard the conversations between him and the Oceanids and Io and demands to know the secret of his downfall. Prometheus defiantly replies that he has already seen two kings overthrown, Uranus and Cronus, and he looks forward to the third, Zeus. Hermes says that no compassion can be expected from Zeus, but Prometheus answers that time teaches all things, including compassion. Hermes predicts that Prometheus' obstinacy will bring him worse torment: Zeus will hurl his thunderbolt and cleave the crag on which he is chained and he will be swallowed up by the mountain; after ages have gone by he will again be set on the crag and an eagle sent by Zeus will tear daily at his liver; and this torture shall be unending unless some god willingly foregòes his immortality and, taking upon himself Prometheus' punishment, descends to the depths of Tartarus forever. The Chorus urges Prometheus to capitulate, but he refuses. The Chorus pledges him their support, and is warned by Hermes of the danger of incurring Zeus' wrath. Hermes departs, and suddenly a violent storm breaks, the crag splits asunder, and Prometheus and the Oceanids sink down into the cliff.

COMMENT: Hermes appears here in his attribute as messenger of the gods, particularly Zeus. His information that Zeus has overheard Prometheus' remarks reflects the Greek belief that Zeus was all-seeing and all-knowing, and therefore did not have to be in a particular place to know what was going on there. Prometheus' statement that time teaches all things seems clearly to look forward to the second and third lost plays of the trilogy, and is one of the major reasons many scholars believe that the trilogy ended with a reconciliation between Zeus and Prometheus. The fact remains that there is no Greek myth depicting Zeus' downfall.

The condition set by Zeus through Hermes for Prometheus' release, that a god be willing to give up his immortality for Prometheus and descend to Tartarus, seems at first glance to be an impossible one. However, Chiron, a Centaur (a creature with a horse's body and a man's head), was accidentally struck by one of Heracles' poisoned arrows, and in order to escape what would otherwise have been never-ending pain he gave up his immortality in favor of Prometheus. Thus, all three of the conditions set for the freeing of Prometheus are ultimately met: since Zeus is never overthrown, he must have become reconciled to Prometheus in order to obtain the Titan's secret concerning Thetis; a descendant of Io, Heracles, did eventually unchain Prometheus; and a god did finally give up his immortality for him.

THE ORESTEIA

(458 B.C.)

BACKGROUND: This is the only complete Greek tragic trilogy extant. Aeschylus won the prize with it. The individual plays are *Agamemnon, The Libation Bearers,* and *The Eumenides.* They were originally followed by a satyr-play, *Proteus,* which has been lost. The first play deals with the murder of Agamemnon, the second with the vengeance of his son Orestes for that murder, and the third with the results of that vengeance. Several years elapse between the first and second plays, and several days between the second and third. The central character of the trilogy as a whole is Orestes, who, though he does not appear in *Agamemnon*, is referred to ominously by both Cassandra and the Chorus. There is no significant character development in any of the individual plays or in the trilogy as a whole.

THEMES: The primary theme of the whole trilogy is the curse of a private blood feud inherited from generation to generation and the necessity of its final replacement by public legal process. Secondary themes involve the concepts that blood once spilled is irrevocable and no really adequate atonement can ever be made; the perpetrator of an evil deed must suffer; one crime leads to other crimes; suffering is inevitable in life, but from suffering comes wisdom; too much worldly success leads to excessive pride and insolence, especially against the gods (hubris), and to eventual ruin and destruction; and that it is not merely worldly success but sin, which is to say hubris, which brings about the ruin.

LEGEND OF THE HOUSE OF ATREUS: The House of Atreus is one of the most famous families in all of Greek mythology. Its story is the prime example of how a blood-feud can lead to an inescapable and continuing curse, which nevertheless can be lifted through expiation and retribution.

Atreus and Thyestes were the sons of Pelops, who was himself the son of Tantalus, and they were fated to be always at odds with one another. When the throne of Mycenae became vacant, the two brothers both claimed it, and at about the same time Thyestes and Atreus' newly married wife, Aerope, conceived a passion for each other. Through a subterfuge Atreus gained the throne and banished his brother. Later, when he discovered that Thyestes had committed adultery with his wife, Atreus became enraged. Soon, however, he thought of a diabolical means of revenge, and so he pretended to forgive Thyestes. He invited his brother to return to Mycenae, promising him amnesty and half of the kingdom. Thyestes accepted. Meanwhile, Atreus captured his brother's sons, Aglaus, Orchomenus, Callileon, and the infant twins, Pleisthenes and Tantalus, and had them murdered. He then hacked all of them limb from limb, had portions of the bodies boiled in a cauldron, and set them before Thyestes at a banquet. After Thyestes had eaten his fill, Atreus sent in the bloody heads, hands, and feet on another platter so that Thyestes could see what he had eaten. Thyestes promptly vomited, and just as promptly laid a perpetual curse upon Atreus and his entire house. He then fled with his one surviving son, Aegisthus. According to some versions of the legend, Thyestes later ordered Aegisthus to kill Atreus, and Aegisthus did. Other versions, however, say that Agamemnon, one of Atreus' sons, drove his father from Mycenae himself. In any case, Agamemnon did in due course become king of Mycenae, and his brother, Menelaus, became king of Sparta. They married the daughters of Tyndareus the Spartan, Clytemnestra and Helen, respectively.

Clytemnestra bore Agamemnon one son, Orestes, and three daughters: Iphigenia, Electra, and Chrysothemis. When Paris, son of Priam, King of Troy, abducted Helen, Agamemnon and Menelaus organized a large army to bring her back by force, and to punish Paris and his people. Aegisthus refused to join the expedition, preferring to remain behind and plot vengeance on the House of Atreus. At Aulis the fleet was becalmed and could not proceed to Troy. The seer Calchas divined that the goddess Artemis had caused the wind to die, and said that she would only be appeased if Agamemnon sacrificed his daughter Iphigenia. Agamemnon reluctantly did so, the wind rose, and the fleet sailed on. During the course of the ten years which the army spent at Troy, Aegisthus became the lover of Clytemnestra, and the two began to plot the murder of Agamemnon when and if he should return. Though Clytemnestra had indeed borne Agamemnon four children, she nonetheless seems to have had little reason to love him very much: he had previously killed her former husband and her new-born child, he had married her by force, though her father had later sanctioned the marriage, he had then gone off to a war which seemed as though it might go on forever, and he had allowed their daughter Iphigenia to be sacrificed at Aulis. Finally, after Troy at last fell in the tenth year of the war, he was reputed to be bringing back with him Cassandra, Priam's daughter, as his mistress. Indeed, it was said, she had already borne him twin sons, Teledamus and Pelops.

Afraid that Agamemnon might return unexpectedly, Clytemnestra wrote him a letter asking him to light a beacon fire on Mount Ida when Troy fell, and she then arranged for a chain of beacons to relay the message to her at Mycenae. To make certain that the signal was not missed, she stationed a watchman on top of the roof of the palace, where he spent a year in watching before the signal finally came.

On the way back from Troy a tremendous storm arose at sea. Many of the ships were sunk, and the rest were widely scattered. Consequently, Agamemnon returned home with only one ship, the one he was on. Clytemnestra greeted her husband with an outward show of delight, unrolled a purple carpet for him, led him to the bathhouse where a bath had been prepared for him, and as he stepped out of the bath threw a net over him. According to some, Aegisthus then killed Agamemnon by stabbing him twice with a double-edged sword. Others, including Aeschylus in his *Agamemnon*, say that Clytemnestra herself did the stabbing. In any case, Clytemnestra then proceeded to hack off her husband's head with an axe, after which she killed Cassandra. Clytemnestra and Aegisthus then ruled in Mycenae.

Electra was subsequently married off to a Mycenaean peasant who, afraid of Orestes and by nature chaste to boot, never consumated the union. Electra acted as a gadfly to Aegisthus and her mother, constantly calling them "murderous adulterers" in public, and continually reminding Orestes of the vengeance required of him. He had been sent away by Clytemnestra before the return of his father, and finally, after either eight or twelve years, he returned determined to kill both Aegisthus and his mother. Before entering the city he visited the Oracle at Delphi to ask whether or not he should destroy his father's murderers. The answer, as usual, was ambiguous. He was told that if he did not avenge Agamemnon he would become an outcast from society, would be prohibited from entering any shrine or temple, and would be afflicted with a leprosy that would eat into his flesh and make it grow a white mold. On the other hand, he was also told that the Furies would not readily be disposed to forgive a matricide, and that they might well pursue and attack him until he was insane or dead, or both. Orestes returned to Mycenae disguised as a traveler bringing news of his own death, and with the help of Electra he gained entry to the palace. When Aegisthus appeared Orestes cut him down with his sword, after which he beheaded his mother. After displaying the bodies to the palace servants, and justifying to them his acts, the serpent-haired, dog-headed, bat-winged Furies appeared and began to beat him with their scourges. Orestes, nearly out of his wits, fled to Delphi to take refuge with Apollo and be purified. There Apollo told him that he must endure an exile of one year, during which he would be constantly tormented by the Furies, but after which he was to go to Athens and embrace the statue of Athene, who would shield him and annul the curse.

Orestes did these things, and after the year, and at the shrine of Athene, Apollo and the Furies appealed to the goddess for a decision. She declined to judge, saying the case was too difficult to be determined by just one person, even if that person were herself. She therefore appointed the Areopagus, a court of Athenian citizens, to hear the arguments and judge the case. After much deliberation, the result was a tie vote, and Athene thereupon cast the deciding ballot in favor of Orestes. He returned to Mycenae, swearing to be a faithful ally of Athens as long as he lived, but the Furies vehemently protested this subverting of the ancient law by upstart gods. They threatened vengeance upon Athens if the verdict were not reversed: to bring barrenness upon the soil, blight the crops, and destroy all the Athenian offspring. Athene pacified them through flattery. She first asserted to them that they were far wiser than herself, and then suggested that they remain in a grotto in Athens where they would gather such multitudes of worshippers as they could never hope to find anywhere else. The Furies, after some consultation, agreed. Thereafter they were known as the Eumenides, the Kindly, or Solemn Ones, a name which Orestes himself was the first to use.

AGAMEMNON

(458 B.C.)

BACKGROUND: This is the first play of the *Oresteia*. It contains little dramatic action. The first half of the play, up to the entrance of Agamemnon, is devoted almost entirely to exposition, preparation, and foreshadowing. The dramatic climax is reached in the verbal dual between Agamemnon and Clytemnestra, the turning point is Agamemnon's surrender to his wife in the matter of walking on the tapestries, and the emotional climax comes with the prophetic ravings of Cassandra and the death cries of Agamemnon, which follow almost at once. The tragic foreboding in and the tragic atmosphere of *Agamemnon* are greater than in any other Greek tragedy.

THEMES: The primary theme of *Agamemnon*, as an individual play, is the vengeance Clytemnestra wreaks upon Agamemnon because, she claims, he sacrificed their daughter, Iphigenia, at Aulis ten years earlier. Secondary themes center on the excessive pride and arrogance (hubris) of Agamemnon, and the hypocrisy, infidelity, and man-like dominance of Clytemnestra. Other themes may be found in the chapter on the *Oresteia*.

CHARACTERS:

WATCHMAN

CLYTEMNESTRA   Wife of King Agamemnon, and mistress to Aegisthus.

HERALD   Messenger who brings an eye-witness account of the events that took place immediately after the conclusion of the Trojan War.

AGAMEMNON   King of Argos and leader of the Greek army during the Trojan War.

CASSANDRA   Daughter of King Priam of Troy, possessed of the gift of prophecy. She became part of the spoils of Agamemnon, and is now his concubine.

AEGISTHUS   Son of Thyestes and cousin of Agamemnon. While Agamemnon was at Troy he became Clytemnestra's lover.

CHORUS OF ARGIVE ELDERS   Senior citizens of Argos.

ATTENDANTS OF CLYTEMNESTRA

ATTENDANTS OF AGAMEMNON   Mute parts.

BODYGUARD OF AEGISTHUS

SETTING: Argos, in northeastern Greece. The action takes place in front of the palace of King Agamemnon. A Watchman is stationed on the roof of the palace. When the play opens it is early in the morning.

> COMMENT: The Watchman is, of course, on the roof of the skene, and although the play was produced in the daylight, the Watchman indicates in the fourth line that he is watching, among other things, "all the stars of night."

PROLOGUE: The Watchman tells how he has been on the roof of the palace, lying dog-like with his head propped on his hands, for a year waiting to see a beacon light flare up in the distance, as a signal that Troy has fallen. He has been ordered there by Clytemnestra, and he is afraid even to sleep for fear he might miss seeing the beacon and thus incur the wrath of his willful queen. Though he says that she has the strength of character of a man, he also complains that the kingdom is no longer being ruled in as fine a way as when Agamemnon was present. He therefore longs for Agamemnon's return. Suddenly a light flares up in the distance; the Watchman hails it as the harbinger of Agamemnon's return, and says how happy he will be to clasp his king's hand again. He is about to comment on the things that have been taking place in the palace, but he bids his tongue to be still; the stones of the palace can tell if they will, but for himself he will be silent. He then leaves to tell Clytemnestra he has seen the beacon light.

COMMENT: The prologue is not spoken by the protagonist, but it nonetheless serves as an admirable opening to the tragedy. The audience is, naturally, aware of the broad outline of the story. Consequently, it knows that the Watchman's joy at the sign that his king will soon return will be short-lived, for Agamemnon is coming home apparently in triumph, but in reality to be murdered. The audience also knows that Clytemnestra has been Aegisthus' mistress during Agamemnon's absence, and that she is not going to greet her husband with true wifely joy. In addition, Aegisthus' primary motive for going to Argos in the first place was to seek revenge upon Agamemnon. Aeschylus has developed dramatic irony in his opening lines, and from this point on virtually everything said by every character in the play will have at least two and sometimes more than two meanings, for the characters are not aware of much that is going to happen, but the audience is.

PARODOS: The Chorus enters and says that ten years have now passed since the departure of Agamemnon and Menelaus, with a great army in a thousand ships, for Troy. They indicate that the war was caused by a breach of hospitality: Paris seduced and carried off Helen while he was a guest in Menelaus' palace. This, in addition to angering the Greeks, angered Zeus as well, for he is, among other things, the protector of hospitality. Therefore Zeus sided with the Greeks in the war, and saw to it that the Trojans were defeated. But the Chorus, though also angry at Paris' deed, was unable to participate in the war for they were already too old at the time, and they lament the fact that they are now ten years older. The Chorus reflects on the inevitability of events: if a law is transgressed, punishment must follow, and the mere offering of libations will not be enough to ward off the punishment; if a war is begun young men must necessarily be killed, for there is no way of preventing death in war.

COMMENT: The Chorus, as a Chorus of Elders, is intended to represent maturity of outlook, experience in the affairs of the world, and a certain amount of objectivity toward the actions of the younger characters in the drama. They indicate that the victory of the Greeks was foreordained, and had little to do with Greek superiority, either in arms or ability. Their reflections inject a cosmic background into the attempted comprehension of men's actions: Agamemnon and Menelaus did not go to war merely because of anger, but also because Zeus incited them; those who were killed in the war and all others who were affected by it were caught up in events beyond their control; man's destiny is something over which he has only limited influence. And these events have a continuing influence, the end of which is not in sight, and is known to no one, for if there had been no Trojan War, Agamemnon would not have been away for ten years; if he had not been away, he would not now be coming home to be murdered by Clytemnestra; if Clytemnestra were not to murder him, she would not be killed in turn by Orestes later, and so on.

FIRST STASIMON: Clytemnestra enters and goes, without speaking, to the altar to pray and offer sacrifices. The Chorus asks her what news she has received that has caused her to do so, and, further, to order sacrifices throughout the city. They wish to know if something has happened that might bring them some comfort after ten long years of war. She does not answer, and while they wait the Chorus reflects on an omen seen before the war began: two eagles, one black and the other with a splash of white, that swooped down upon a hare swollen with unborn young and tore it to pieces. The soothsayer Calchas had said that the eagles represented the two sons of Atreus, the hare Troy, and the unborn young the inhabitants of Troy. But Calchas also warned the Greeks against angering the gods in any way in the conduct of the war, saying that Artemis in particular was jealous of the House of Atreus and was waiting for an opportunity to bring catastrophe upon it. Calchas then prayed to Apollo to prevent Artemis from becalming the Greek ships at Aulis, thereby forcing a new, unholy sacrifice, especially since potential wrath, in the form of Clytemnestra, is lurking in the palace. The Chorus remarks that the prophecy of Calchas appeared to be basically good, but that the seeds of evil and sorrow were also present. Nonetheless, they hope, at line 159, that good will "win out in the end." The Chorus states that it has been unsuccessfully seeking a solution to the mystery of Calchas' prophecy, and it calls upon neither Uranus or Cronus, since their power is at an end, but upon Zeus, as the only one capable of giving an answer, for aid.

At this point the Chorus pauses to meditate upon one of the supreme mysteries and ironies of life: Zeus has made it possible, indeed has ordained, that man gain knowledge. Yet every time Zeus intervenes or interferes in the life of man, sorrow results. Furthermore, man himself, without any influence from the gods, is apt to transgress the divine law, and this brings inevitable retribution. And every crime breeds new crimes, and so the suffering of man is compounded. Consequently, though man achieves knowledge, Zeus has seen to it that it is gained only through suffering. This fact, concludes the Chorus, is not to be, and cannot be, fought; it must be accepted with resignation.

Now the Chorus tells of the Greek fleet becalmed at Aulis, the statement by Calchas that Artemis was indeed offended and would not send favorable winds until Agamemnon sacrificed Iphigenia to her, the reluctance of Agamemnon either to sacrifice his daughter or to allow the expedition to fail, and his final decision to have the deed performed despite Iphigenia's pleas for mercy and her attempt to lay a curse upon the House of Atreus. The final outcome of this sacrifice is not yet known, concludes the Chorus, for it lies still in the future.

COMMENT: There was always an altar at the center of the orchestra of every Greek theatre. It is at this altar that Clytemnestra offers her sacrifice.

The recounting by the Chorus of the events at Aulis, and its meditation on knowledge and suffering, allow it to present some of Aeschylus' key ideas. Man lives his life in constant contact with other men, and he is therefore affected by the actions of other men. He is also affected by the actions of the gods, particularly Zeus. Therefore, since so many outside forces are influencing him, man has relatively little control over his own life and actions. In addition, most of the things that influence man bring about his unhappiness. As a result, life is basically tragic. Nevertheless, there is a value to suffering, for through it man attains wisdom, and without wisdom life, unhappy as it is, would be even more unhappy.

Agamemnon is living proof of this. Through the combined acts of Zeus, Paris, Helen, and others, he has to decide whether or not to go to war. Having decided affirmatively, he finds himself and his fleet stranded at Aulis. He is forced there to make a choice between two equally distasteful alternatives: to order the sacrifice of his daughter, or to call off the expedition, for without the sacrifice Artemis will not permit the ships to continue toward Troy. He clearly indicates his love for Iphigenia and his aversion to sacrificing her, yet he does choose to sacrifice her because of his proud desire to be a great military leader and conqueror. It is important to bear in mind that though Agamemnon did not create the alternatives, he nonetheless did choose between them of his own free will, and that many other events have been flowing and are continuing to flow from that choice. For example, had he chosen differently, he would have had to return home with his army, he would not have conquered and sacked Troy, and he would not now be about to be murdered. Perhaps Agamemnon has learned nothing from all of this, but at least the people around him and in the audience have an opportunity to do so.

FIRST EPISODE: The Chorus again asks Clytemnestra why she has been making sacrifices, and implores her to say if she has received good news. She tells them that Troy has fallen, and they receive the news with joy but wonder how she came to know it. She tells them about the series of signal fires that conveyed the message to the Watchman and thence to her, and goes on to describe vividly what she imagines to be the plight of the conquered Trojans. Then she prays that the Greeks, while sacking the city, give due reverence to the gods and not anger them by damaging or destroying any of their temples, for if they do the gods will be certain to wreak their own vengeance. The Chorus prepares to offer thanksgiving to the gods for the Greek victory.

COMMENT: Here an aspect of the "masculine character" of Clytemnestra is further developed. Only a strong-willed person possessed of outstanding organizational ability would be able to create such a system of beacons and make it work. Also, there is a certain amount of irony in her prayers that no evil befall the Greeks, for she is herself planning to act evilly toward Agamemnon, and she might have great difficulty doing so if he were to return at the head of a victorious army. Significantly, of course, when he does return, it is with only one shipload of men.

SECOND STASIMON: The Chorus sings in praise of Zeus, guardian of hospitality, who punished Troy for the vaunting sin of Paris. Great pride always will be punished. Helen, too, contributed to the downfall of Troy. When she "stepped forth lightly between the gates daring beyond all daring," she took with her a dowry of destruction. Prophets predicted the great catastrophe, pointing out that Menelaus would be unable to bear the barrenness of his bed. Yet the catastrophe was to be Greek as well as Trojan, for innumerable homes would have empty beds after the men went off to Troy, and the beds of many whose ashes would return in urns would remain empty. And all this for a woman. It is almost too much to bear. The people of Greece hate the war and believe that the gods will punish the House of Atreus for its excessive pride and desire for revenge, glory, and wealth which led to so much death and destruction.

COMMENT: The Chorus here describes the sin of hubris as it applies to Paris and the House of Atreus, particularly Agamemnon, who was the leader of the Greek forces. Agamemnon, through his thirst for power and glory, violated the concept of sôphrosynê, or moderation. The audience, therefore, is being prepared for his downfall. In addition to the negative things that have been said about him thus far in the play, they would also remember that Homer had shown in the *Iliad* how Agamemnon's dispute with Achilles over yet another woman, the captured Briseis, had led to Achilles' withdrawal of himself and his Myrmidons from the fighting and the consequent prolongation of the war and its agonies. Homer's attitude toward Agamemnon was not as negative as that of Aeschylus, but the *Iliad* had been composed some three centuries earlier, and in the meantime Greek civilization had developed and evolved and Greek attitudes and ideals had changed as well.

Interestingly, Aeschylus also points here to another fact of life: when a great sin is committed by an important member of a society (or a city), in this case first Paris and then Agamemnon, the punishment will usually involve the entire society.

SECOND EPISODE: The Chorus comments on the speed with which the news transmitted by the beacon has swept the city, but wonders, since no confirming message has arrived from Troy, if the beacon might have been false. It is true that Clytemnestra believes it, but they assert that women are noted for believing things before they are proven. Suddenly a Herald appears. He is an advance messenger from Agamemnon's forces which have just landed, and wears an olive wreath in token of victory. He first gives thanks for being able to return to his beloved land after having virtually given up hope of being able to die there rather than before Troy. He then calls upon all to give royal greetings to Agamemnon, who is returning victorious. Almost in passing he mentions that Agamemnon, in totally destroying Troy, also destroyed all of the Trojan temples and shrines, and he again praises Agamemnon for having caused the Trojans to suffer twice as much as necessary for Paris' crime. The Chorus cautiously indicates that there have been problems at home during the absence of Agamemnon and the army, but the Herald does not understand what is being said. He goes on to describe the tribulations, suffering, and indeed misery of the army during its ten years at Troy, and tells how thankful the survivors are to have been able to return in victory, and also alive. Clytemnestra chides the Chorus for having believed neither the beacon nor her interpretation of it, and for considering her to be weakly womanly. She then directs the Herald to greet Agamemnon for her, and tell him that she has been loving and faithful in his absence. The Chorus implies to the Herald that there is more to her words than meets the eye, and asks if Menelaus is also returning with Agamemnon. The Herald tells of a furious storm which struck the Greek fleet on its way home and left only Agamemnon's ship in sight, having sunk or scattered all the rest.

COMMENT: Great sin is followed by a great downfall, but before there can be great sin there must be a great sinner. And before one can be a great sinner one must have greatness of stature. In *Agamemnon* two characters are shown to have tremendous stature, and they both become great sinners: Agamemnon and Clytemnestra. Some of Agamemnon's stupendous feats have already been alluded to by the Chorus, and more are spoken of now by the Herald. Strikingly, however, they are feats which have the seeds of disaster within them as well as the seeds of glory. The audience is now being prepared for the enormous evil to be perpetrated by Clytemnestra, and she is being given a stature comparable to her husband's. She has already acted and ruled with the strength of character of a man, and now she plays the hypocrite in front of the elders of the city, brazening out her lies about her love for and fidelity to Agamemnon. The members of the Chorus made clear to the Herald, before Clytemnestra said a word, that they knew all about what was going on between herself and Aegisthus; indeed, the entire city knows about it, for who could fail to be aware of it? Yet Clytemnestra is confident the Chorus will say nothing specific to denounce her, and she is right. Agamemnon, the protagonist, has in Clytemnestra an antagonist worthy of him.

This Episode is also significant for the description of the army given by the Herald. He tells no romantic tales of war; there are no dashing heroes, no gallant battles, no delightful interludes. He describes ten years of discomfort, suffering and woe. This contributes to the overall feeling of gloom and doom that pervades the tragedy, and it gives further evidence of the guilt incurred by Agamemnon in the waging of what was essentially an unjust war.

THIRD STASIMON: The Chorus ponders the name of Helen, saying that she must have received her name from one of the gods, for the meaning of her name is death: death to ships, men, and cities. They tell a story of a man who raised a lion cub in his house. When the cub was young it cavorted and played with the family like a kitten, but when it matured it slaughtered the man's flocks and his family as well. This, they say, is comparable to the story of Helen, who when she first arrived at Troy gave pleasure to Paris and the Trojans, but eventually brought about their destruction. It has been said, they go on, that wealth and good fortune bring about evil, but this is not so. Hubris—excessive pride and arrogance—causes evil, and brings on justice through retribution. Blessings and happiness come to those who are humble and righteous. And they repeat that crime breeds crime, even though at times the seed of evil may lie dormant.

> **COMMENT:** The Chorus further develops ideas which it has previously presented. Interestingly, it says that wealth in itself does not bring about evil, but that excessive wealth predisposes the possessor to evil. Consequently, Righteousness tends to avoid the houses of the rich, and dwells instead in the houses of the poor and simple in heart.

THIRD EPISODE: Agamemnon enters in a chariot, and accompanied by a procession. Cassandra is at his side. The Chorus attempts to find a suitable manner of greeting him, neither too excessive nor too restrained. They point out to him that they were not in favor of the war, and were unhappy when he mounted the expedition. Nonetheless, they are now pleased that he has returned victorious. They tell him that he will learn soon enough who in the city were loyal and who faithless. Agamemnon replies that before doing anything else he must go to the temples to give thanks to the gods for giving the victory to the Greeks. Because of the transgression of one woman, "the beast of Argos," "a wild and bloody lion," leaped upon Troy and utterly destroyed it. He asserts that he knows well enough that people envy power, wealth, and success, for he has experienced disloyalty during the ten years of war, and he praises Odysseus, who had accompanied the expedition reluctantly, as the only one who was loyal and steadfast throughout. But, he says, the determining of loyalties at home can wait until after he has entered his palace, thanked the gods, and refreshed himself.

> **COMMENT:** The words of the Chorus are more ironic than it realizes, for Agamemnon will learn more quickly than the Chorus suspects of the disloyalty of Clytemnestra. Additionally, Agamemnon's words are more ironic than he realizes. First, he has unknowingly echoed the tale of the Chorus about the man and the lion, likening the Greek army to a ravening lion that destroyed Troy. Second, he has clearly indicated his own arrogant hubris, for while he gives credit to the gods for the victory, he appropriates the glory to himself. His pride of self is so great that he brushes aside the Chorus' warning, feeling that his

mere presence is enough to cast fear into the hearts of those who were unfaithful, and thus render them impotent until he in his own good time should choose to punish them.

Clytemnestra comes forward and declares her love for Agamemnon. She depicts the sufferings a faithful wife must endure when her husband goes off to war: sleepless nights, rumors of his death, fear of betrayal in his absence, thoughts of suicide. She says Orestes is not present to greet his father because she became fearful for his life and sent him away for his protection. Then she directs her handmaidens to strew crimson and purple tapestries between the chariot and the palace so that Agamemnon's feet need not touch the earth. He is to enter his house "where Justice leads him," on "a crimson path." Agamemnon wryly remarks that his wife's greeting has been almost as long as his own absence, and objects to the tapestries. Such state is suitable only for gods, and would be sacrilegious for a man. Clytemnestra urges that since he is the great victor of Troy, he might well allow her to be victorious in this, and he accedes with little further argument. He has his sandals removed and offers the weakly pious hope that no god will be offended at his extravagance. Then he asks that Cassandra be treated kindly; no slave bears the yoke willingly, and the gods watch to see the conqueror who uses his power with restraint and justice. Clytemnestra arrogantly declares that she would have trampled innumerable such tapestries if she thought it would have brought her husband home sooner, and she and Agamemnon enter the palace. She says nothing whatever about Cassandra.

COMMENT: This is certainly the central section of the tragedy, and virtually everything said is highly ironic. When Clytemnestra speaks of her love for Agamemnon, she is being deliberately ironic; she knows that he will assume she is speaking truthfully, but she also knows the Chorus is fully aware of the real nature of her "love," and assumes they will remain silent about it. She is right, as she is with her story of the faithful wife. Certainly such a wife would be affected in the way she describes, but the Chorus and the audience are aware that she was neither faithful nor so affected. It is true that she sent Orestes away, but she did so because of fear of him, not for him. And when she speaks of Agamemnon entering where Justice leads him on a crimson path, she means her justice which will lead him to a path crimson with his blood. Agamemnon, when he refuses to walk on the tapestries, shows intelligence and nobility, but when he agrees to do so gives immediate, concrete evidence of his hubris. It is noteworthy that although this is the only time in the tragedy that Agamemnon, the protagonist, appears on stage (in fact, the only character to appear more than once is Clytemnestra), he nevertheless dominates the play. It is quite clearly his fate which is prepared for before his appearance, and his fate which controls the actions of the other characters even after his death. Aeschylus was completely correct when he named the drama after Agamemnon, rather than after Clytemnestra.

FOURTH STASIMON: Cassandra has remained in the chariot, and the Chorus meditates on the ambiguity of Agamemnon's homecoming. It should be an occasion of great joy and celebration, and yet they are filled with a sense of foreboding for what the future will bring.

COMMENT: Agamemnon, of course, had to enter the palace alone so that his hubris could be shown directly and without any distraction. Cassandra has to remain behind temporarily so that she can later utter her prophetic warnings concerning her own and Agamemnon's fates. The Chorus here gives advance counterpoint to those warnings.

FOURTH EPISODE: Clytemnestra comes out of the palace and tells Cassandra to go inside, and remarks how fortunate Cassandra is to be coming as a slave to a household that knows so well how to treat her. Cassandra refuses to answer or to move, and the Chorus urges her to obey, declaring that when a person is trapped in the net of slavery he is at the mercy of the master. Cassandra still does not move or speak, and Clytemnestra goes back into the palace in anger. Cassandra now bursts forth into wildly prophetic and enigmatic expressions. She recalls the past unsavory history of the House of Atreus and prophecies the murder of Agamemnon by Clytemnestra. She describes Agamemnon as being snared in a "net of death," and being slain by Clytemnestra, but the Chorus cannot comprehend the meaning of her words. The Chorus declares that nothing but sorrow has ever come from prophecies and that this time will be no different, and can divine nothing but madness in Cassandra's ravings. She speaks further of the curse placed upon the House of Atreus, and the Chorus is amazed that she, an alien, should know its history so completely. She tells how she obtained her prophetic powers: in return for the gift from Apollo she promised to become his mistress; she broke her promise and Apollo decreed that no one would ever believe her prophecies. She repeats her prophecy of Agamemnon's slaying, and goes on to predict her own murder at the hands of Clytemnestra. She adds that these killings will not go unavenged, that there is one who is now an "outlaw and wanderer" who was "born to slay his mother, and to wreak death for his father's blood." She now is finished with prophecy, for her life is about to end, so she casts aside her staff and circlet of flowers, the symbols of a seer. She resigns herself to and accepts her fate, and goes slowly into the palace. The Chorus again indicates its lack of comprehension. Suddenly Agamemnon's agonized voice is heard from inside the palace. He cries out that he has been stabbed once, then twice. The Chorus dashes about distractedly, unable to decide what to do, or even if anything should be done.

COMMENT: Dramatic irony is again quite evident. Clytemnestra well knows the kind of treatment her household will give Cassandra, and Cassandra herself is well aware of it. So is the audience, but the Chorus is completely in the dark. During the scene a dual-leveled conversation takes place. The Chorus talks to Cassandra, but she only partly talks to them, for much of the time she talks primarily to Apollo. It is really no wonder that the Chorus does not understand her. The one who was "born to slay his mother" is, of course, Orestes, though his name is never mentioned by Cassandra. Significantly, a net is mentioned three times, once by the Chorus and twice by Cassandra. The Chorus, speaking of a net of slavery, is referring to Cassandra's being caught in that net, but they are also unknowingly prefiguring Agamemnon's death. Cassandra uses the word to describe specifically that death, but the meaning of her words is not grasped by the Chorus.

EXODOS: The doors of the palace are thrown open to reveal the bodies of Agamemnon and Cassandra, with Clytemnestra, blood smeared on her, standing over them. She triumphantly describes how she cast a net over her husband, much as a fisherman would cast one over a fish, and struck him two deadly blows; then, after he fell, she struck him a third time. She had to do much dissembling until this time, but now that she has done the deed she had long planned, and she has been made happy by having Agamemnon's blood splash on her, she can speak the truth without concern. The Chorus is dumbfounded, and begins to condemn her, but she promptly orders them to be silent or she will banish them from the city. And if they attempt to punish her, they will be killed. She then accuses the Chorus of hypocrisy. Where were their accusations when Agamemnon slaughtered his own child? There were none. And where was their punishment of him? There was none. So now, she says, be still. The Chorus warns her of inevitable Justice to come, but she declares that she herself has been the tool of Justice. She has punished Agamemnon for slaying their daughter, and also for sharing his bed with Cassandra. She fears no Justice, especially since she has Aegisthus to defend her. In a further exchange she asserts that she has also been a tool for the working out of the curse that was placed on the House of Atreus, and therefore on Agamemnon.

The Chorus asks who shall bury and mourn Agamemnon, and Clytemnestra replies that though she who killed him will bury him, she will shed no tears over him. If anyone is to greet him and forgive him in death it must be Iphigenia, and she prays that the curse on the House will go with him. Indeed, she says she would be content with only a part of the House's wealth if only it would be freed of its curse of slaughter following upon slaughter. Aegisthus now enters accompanied by his bodyguard. He exults over the slaying of Agamemnon, and recounts his own reasons for wanting him dead: the murder of his brothers by Agamemnon's father, and the serving of their flesh to his own father. The Chorus threatens Aegisthus with retribution, and he chides them for being old men incapable of anything. The Chorus, after condemning Aegisthus for having sat out the war and lurking in the palace to wait for Agamemnon's return, and then, coward that he was, allowing a woman to do his deed, is about to draw swords against him and his bodyguard, when Clytemnestra intervenes. There has been enough killing, she says, and when the Chorus calls upon Orestes to return to avenge his father's murder and rid the city of Clytemnestra and

Aegisthus, she dismisses their words as impotent ravings. For, she declares, she and Aegisthus are now in control of the city.

COMMENT: Clytemnestra and the bodies of Agamemnon and Cassandra are revealed in a tableau on the eccyclema, which is wheeled out through the center doors of the skene. Since it would be very difficult, and extremely undignified, for the actor portraying Clytemnestra to climb down off the eccyclema, all of her lines in this scene are delivered from there.

The image Clytemnestra presents of a fisherman netting a fish to point up the way she enmeshed Agamemnon is tremendously effective. Agamemnon was about to step out of the bath full of water when Clytemnestra, approaching as if to wrap a towel about him, threw over his head a net garment which she had woven herself, and which had no neck or arm openings. Agamemnon became entangled like a fish and was easily stabbed to death. In the *Odyssey*, Homer comments on the striking differences between Clytemnestra and Penelope and the homecomings they provided their husbands. Penelope spent the last three years of Odysseus' absence weaving a shroud for her father-in-law, Laertes, unraveling at night what she had woven during the day so that she would not have to fulfill her promise to choose a second husband when the shroud was finished. (Fortunately, Laertes did not die until after Odysseus returned.) Clytemnestra also spent time weaving during Agamemnon's absence, but she wove the net robe in which she was planning to kill him. In addition, she gave herself to Aegisthus.

Clytemnestra presents a three-fold justification for her act. First, she is a mother avenging the slaying of her child, Iphigenia. Second, she is a wife (and a jealous one, at that) avenging her betrayal with Cassandra by her husband. Third, she is the instrument of the gods in the working out of the curse placed upon the House of Atreus. Her arguments are strong and forceful, as well they might be, since such cold-blooded bitterness is obviously the result of years of carefully nursed hatred, but they are not convincing. She herself, with Aegisthus, has betrayed her husband in his absence, and she is intoxicated by the power and authority she has exercised while he was away. Her justification is as significant for what it omits as for what it contains.

The almost total ineffectiveness of the Chorus in this scene is to be expected, for Aeschylus has carefully prepared for it. The Chorus is introduced early in the tragedy as a group of old men, and they have described themselves as "no stronger than a child." Their simple-mindedness and lack of insight in the scene with Cassandra also prepares for their weakness and indecision here. And when they finally resolve to fight with Aegisthus and his men, they are easily quelled by a few words from Clytemnestra.

Aegisthus' almost hysterical reaction to the words of the Chorus, combined with his having to appear with a bodyguard at his back, effectively point up his basic cowardice and lack of character. It is Clytemnestra who is strong, not Aegisthus, and the audience is left to infer that without her he would never have been able to have revenged himself on Agamemnon.

THE LIBATION BEARERS
(Choephroe)

(458 B.C.)

BACKGROUND: *The Libation Bearers* (*Choephroe*) is the second play of the *Oresteia*. Considerable time has passed between the murder of Agamemnon and the action of *The Libation Bearers*, perhaps as much as the seven years indicated in the *Odyssey*. Nowhere in the text of the play, however, is there any precise statement on this point. Clytemnestra and Aegisthus still rule; Electra, Orestes' sister, is now a young woman; and Orestes, as the play opens, has just returned with his best friend, Pylades, to avenge his father's murder. This is the first extant play to contain a recognition scene, and though the manner by which Electra concludes that Orestes has been at Agamemnon's grave is rather implausible, playwrights were just beginning to use a technique which is difficult in itself. This is also the first extant play to contain the type of intrigue in which the protagonist reveals to a third party (in this case the Chorus) a deed which he plans to commit and the manner in which he itends to perform it (here the murder of Clytemnestra).

THEMES: The primary theme of *The Libation Bearers*, as an individual play, is the revenge of Orestes upon his mother and Aegisthus for the murder of Agamemnon. According to the law of the blood feud, this revenge was Orestes' foremost obligation. The slaying of a parent, however, is also a crime against nature, and would normally lead to the necessity of another member of the family avenging it. Partly because this is impossible, and partly because of the enormity of the crime of matricide, the Furies become the avengers, and the manner in which they are placated is the subject of the third play of the trilogy, *The Eumenides*. Secondary themes are referred to in the chapter on the *Oresteia*.

CHARACTERS:

ORESTES   Son of Agamemnon and Clytemnestra and brother of Electra.

PYLADES   Friend of Orestes.

ELECTRA   Daughter of Agamemnon and Clytemnestra and sister of Orestes.

CHORUS   Slave women brought by Agamemnon from Troy.

A SERVANT   A doorkeeper.

CLYTEMNESTRA   Queen of Argos. Formerly the wife of Agamemnon, now the wife of Aegisthus. Mother of Orestes and Electra.

CILISSA   Nurse of Orestes when he was a child.

AEGISTHUS   Cousin of Orestes, now husband of Clytemnestra and King of Argos.

A FOLLOWER OF AEGISTHUS

ATTENDANTS OF ORESTES

ATTENDANTS OF CLYTEMNESTRA   } Mute parts.

ATTENDANTS OF AEGISTHUS

SETTING: Argos, in northeastern Greece. The action of a little more than the first half of the play takes place at the tomb of Agamemnon; the balance in front of Clytemnestra's palace. The play opens in the early morning, and night is falling by the time Orestes arrives at the palace.

> **COMMENT:**   The altar in the center of the orchestra represents the tomb of Agamemnon, so that although the scene changes midway in the tragedy, no mechanical change takes place.

PROLOGUE: Orestes and Pylades enter disguised as travelers and approach the altar and tomb of Agamemnon. Orestes places two locks of his hair on the tomb. One, he says, is in honor of Inachus, who raised him to manhood; the other honors his father, for whose death and funeral he had not been present. He prays to Hermes to protect him, and to his father to hear him. The Chorus and Electra enter, clothed in black. Orestes prays to Zeus to aid him in avenging his father's murder, recognizes his sister Electra, and takes Pylades aside so they can observe without being seen or recognized.

> COMMENT: The first part of the Prologue is missing in the manuscripts, but it is probable that in that section Orestes revealed the command of Apollo to him to avenge his father's murder. In any case, he considers the taking of vengeance to be an inescapable obligation. Inachus was the god of the river of the same name, and was reputed to have been the founder of the city of Argos. Hermes was, among other things, the god of everything involving dexterity and cunning. In his capacity as messenger of the gods it was his duty to lead the shades of the dead to the underworld. He was also the protector of men in dangerous undertakings. It is therefore obvious why Orestes implores his aid.

PARODOS: The Chorus, carrying vessels for libation, says that they have been ordered by Clytemnestra to offer libations for Agamemnon. They lament his death and the current situation in Argos. Clytemnestra has had an ominous dream which revealed that the dead were full of wrath for their murderers. The Chorus also laments their own enslavement, and says that they have been rending their clothes and their faces because of it. They go on to say that libations are not enough to prevent vengeance; nothing can wash off blood once it has been shed, crime will follow crime, murder will follow murder. They then mourn the fall of Troy and the necessity of their being slaves in a household whose masters, Clytemnestra and Aegisthus, they hate.

> COMMENT: The Chorus is careful not to reveal too many of the details of Clytemnestra's dream at this point; the rest are given later in the play. It is clear, however, that Clytemnestra is afraid of retribution, and is trying to avoid it through the offering of libations. It is also clear, as the

Chorus points out, that retribution cannot be avoided, for one crime breeds another and that one still others. In addition, the curse laid on the House of Atreus by Thyestes necessitates that one murder must follow upon another. Since the Chorus is made up of Trojan women who were brought back by Agamemnon as captives, it is natural that they should lament their condition. Their complaints also indicate that Clytemnestra and Aegisthus have been oppressive rulers.

FIRST EPISODE: Electra, before offering the libation, ironically asks the Chorus whether she is really to be expected to do so in her mother's name, and, if so, how can she pray that her father return good to the woman who murdered him? Perhaps it would be better if she simply emptied the vessel onto the ground like so much refuse. She asks the Chorus to be frank in answering, for they all share the same hatred toward Clytemnestra and Aegisthus. In a series of alternating lines the Chorus advises Electra to pray for those who love Agamemnon, beginning with herself first; for those who hate Aegisthus, beginning with themselves; for the one who wanders in exile, Orestes; and for someone, man or god, to come and kill Clytemnestra and Aegisthus. Electra thereupon prays to Hermes and to her father's shade to aid her, slave and outcast in her own house, and Orestes, an exile from his own home. And she asks that Orestes be allowed to return home, and that an avenger be sent to kill Clytemnestra and Aegisthus, both of whom were responsible for Agamemnon's murder.

The Chorus repeats Electra's prayer for an avenger, and then she suddenly sees the two locks of hair left by Orestes. She examines one, and in another series of alternating lines, concludes with the Chorus that because it matches her own hair so closely, and because only she and Orestes would wish to grace her father's tomb in this way, it must therefore be her brother's, sent by him to do their father honor. Yet the sign is inconclusive, and she has doubts. Then she spies the footprints made by Orestes and Pylades, measures her brother's print with her own, notes the similarity, and is almost convinced he has been there, though a doubt still lingers in her mind. Suddenly Orestes comes from his hiding-place and reveals himself to his sister, matching the lock to his own hair and drawing Electra's attention to the robe he is wearing, a robe which she herself had woven for him. She greets him with a fourfold outpouring of love: the love she would bear her father were he alive, the love she would bear her mother were she worthy of it, the love she would bear her sister Iphigenia were she alive, and the love she quite naturally bears her brother who is now with her again.

Orestes calls upon Zeus to protect himself and his sister, children of the eagle-father, for, if they are destroyed, who will then give homage to Zeus as their father did? The Chorus urges silence and caution lest someone overhear and betray them all to Clytemnestra and Aegisthus, but Orestes goes on to state that he has been specifically commanded by Apollo to avenge Agamemnon's murder. He adds that Apollo's oracle also said that if he did not avenge his father he would himself be tormented and punished by Furies sent by Agamemnon. He asks how he could possibly doubt such oracles, and adds that even if he did disbelieve them he would still have an inner compulsion to wreak vengeance. He is the son of his father, who conquered Troy, and he will not give up his heritage and his estate to what he contemptuously describes as a pair of women Aegisthus, he says, may have the form of a man, but he has the heart of a woman, for he is a coward.

> **COMMENT:** Electra, as portrayed by Aeschylus, is usual-
> ly thought to be a rather weak character compared to the
> manner in which she is depicted by both Sophocles and
> Euripides in their plays entitled *Electra*. In those plays she
> appears as a true daughter of Clytemnestra, overflowing
> with the desire and venom of vengeance. Aeschylus pre-
> sents her as being perhaps more womanly than do the
> other two dramatists. She is somewhat ironic in asking the
> Chorus for advice, but nevertheless she does ask. The
> Chorus also finds it necessary to remind her of Orestes,
> and the manner in which she compares her own and her
> brother's footprints does seem to add to the impression of
> a somewhat simple nature. Still, during the course of this
> Episode and the following Kommos she does work herself
> up into a strong and savage fury, which in itself is not at
> all indicative of weakness. Unfortunately, this fury finds
> no further outlet in the play, because these are the only

scenes in which Electra appears, and this fact no doubt contributes strongly to the ambiguity many feel regarding her.

The Chorus is intriguing because the members play a direct part in the action of this scene. Usually a Chorus offers opinions or advice and is ignored by the other characters, but here it is the Chorus which urges Electra not to pray and to pour the libation not for her mother's benefit but for her own, her brother's, and theirs; she follows their urging. In fact, Electra accepts practically all of the advice the Chorus gives her, and it is only after Orestes reveals himself that the Chorus reverts to its more usual role.

The alternating line-by-line conversations are known as *stichomythia*. This is an unwieldy technique and one which by Aeschylus' time was already considered to be archaic. It dates back to the beginnings of drama when the leader of the Chorus stood apart and conversed with the Chorus proper. Aeschylus obviously felt it necessary to have Electra talk to the Chorus here, and chose this rather formalistic manner of accomplishing his aim, but its effectiveness is somewhat debatable.

Electra asserts that both Clytemnestra and Aegisthus murdered Agamemnon. Some versions of the legend of the House of Atreus say that Clytemnestra threw the net over Agamemnon, and Aegisthus then stabbed him twice, after which Clytemnestra cut off his head with an axe. In *Agamemnon,* Aeschylus has Clytemnestra claim that she alone threw the net over and killed her husband. (See the chapter on the *Oresteia.*) It really doesn't matter too much, because the sole reason for Aegisthus' presence in Argos was to bring about his vengeance on Agamemnon, and his mere presence in the palace, if not in the room, at the time of Agamemnon's murder is enough to make him equally guilty of the crime.

Recognition scenes became a fairly common staple of Greek tragedy, and their technique came to exhibit considerably more finesse than this one. As mentioned in the Background to this play, however, *The Libation Bearers* is the earliest surviving play to utilize such a scene, and this probably helps to explain its awkwardness. Aeschylus, great dramatist though he was, was nonetheless unable to do everything perfectly.

Orestes calls his sister and himself children of the eagle-father. In *Agamemnon* the Chorus had told of an omen seen before the beginning of the Trojan War, an omen in which two eagles had torn to pieces a hare and her unborn young. The eagles represented Agamemnon and Menelaus, and Agamemnon was therefore the eagle-father of Orestes and Electra.

The Furies were the supernatural avengers of parricide, matricide, and perjury, and they were normally called upon by the victim to wreak vengeance on the perpetrator of the crime. Orestes is faced, consequently, with a tragic dilemma, for if he refuses to follow Apollo's injunction to avenge his father, Agamemnon will call upon them to attack him, and if he does take vengeance, his mother will invoke them to do the same thing. This is another example of the Greek feeling that life consists of a series of equally impossible choices, but that man nevertheless has to make choices and do the best he can.

Orestes' comments about Aegisthus remind the audience that Aegisthus did not participate in the Trojan War and has consistently played second fiddle to Clytemnestra, who, though a woman, is more of a man than he is.

KOMMOS (FIRST STASIMON): Orestes, Electra, and the Chorus gather around the tomb of Agamemnon and pray to the Fates, Zeus, and Agamemnon. The Chorus asks the Fates and Zeus to implement the vengeance Orestes has just said (at the end of the First Episode) was ordered of him by Apollo, for Justice demands blood for blood. They all chant lamentations of Agamemnon. How much better it would have been if he had been killed before Troy; he would have died a hero and would have been honored by both the living in Greece and the dead in Hades. And he would have received a burial befitting his nobility and stature. As it was, Clytemnestra buried him ignobly, not even permitting the citizens of Argos to mourn him publicly. Since then Electra has been treated more like a servant than the daughter of the house, and Orestes has been denied

his inheritance. Orestes swears to kill his mother, Electra
swears to help him, and the Chorus swears to help them both.

> **COMMENT:** A *kommos* consists of a series of alternating
> passages of dialogue, usually between the protagonist and
> the chorus. In this kommos Orestes (the protagonist),
> Electra, and the Chorus all participate. A kommos takes
> the place of a stasimon. This kommos serves to show the
> heightened emotional fervor and final commitment of all
> to the intended revenge.

SECOND EPISODE: Orestes and Electra call upon their father
to rise from Hades and aid them in their vengeance, but he
does not appear. The Chorus states that the lamentations and
prayers of Orestes and Electra have been most worthy, but
now the time for action has come. Orestes agrees, but says that
first he would like to know why Clytemnestra sent libations;
even if the offering of all one possessed could atone for a blood
crime, which it could not, his mother is the last person he
would expect to attempt atonement in the first place. The Chorus replies that Clytemnestra had a dream in which she gave
birth to a snake, clothed it like a baby, and when it was hungry
suckled it, and the serpent bit her breast, drawing forth blood
with the milk. She feared that the dream was an ill omen, and
sent the offerings in the hope they would counteract it. Orestes
says the snake is himself; he was born of Clytemnestra,
wrapped in clothes by her, and suckled by her, and the blood
indicates clearly that he is to kill her. The Chorus agrees with
this interpretation, and asks Orestes how he intends to accom-
plish his purpose. He answers that Electra must return to the
palace, maintaining secrecy about her brother's return. Thus
those who murdered his father through treachery shall themselves be killed by treachery. Orestes and his friend Pylades
will approach the palace, disguised as travelers and affecting
the Parnassian dialect, and after being admitted Orestes will
take the first opportunity to slay Aegisthus. The Chorus must
either be silent or speak in a way that will aid Orestes' vengeance.

> **COMMENT:** Although in *The Persians* the ghost of Darius
> and in *The Eumenides* the ghost of Clytemnestra appear,
> here, even though invoked by his children, the ghost of
> Agamemnon does not appear. This non-appearance is sty-

listically quite important, for the Chorus is immediately able to step in and point out that the time for lamentation and prayer is at an end and the time for action is at hand. Obviously, if Agamemnon's ghost had materialized we would have a quite different play.

As mentioned in the Background to this play, the intrigue which takes place in this Episode is the earliest surviving example of a technique which was later used by dramatists with even greater success.

Orestes anticipates little difficulty in being admitted to the palace, for the Greek concept of hospitality required that travelers be fed, sheltered, and well-treated generally. He speaks generally of killing both Clytemnestra and Aegisthus, but at the end of the Episode mentions only Aegisthus by name. This is not an oversight; he intends to kill Aegisthus first and take care of Clytemnestra afterward. Thus the major killing, that of his mother, will be the climax of his vengeance.

SECOND STASIMON: Many and many are the horrors of the earth, says the Chorus: sea-monsters, lightning, meteors, demons, whirlwinds; yet none are as terrible as a woman consumed by passion and wrath. By way of examples they mention Althea, Scylla, and the women of Lemnos. But, they add, Justice pursued and punished all of these women just as, through Orestes, it will punish Clytemnestra.

COMMENT: This stasimon serves as a transition between the departure of Orestes and Pylades from Agamemnon's tomb and their appearance outside the palace in the next episode. The action is not advanced, but the anticipation of the audience is heightened by the Chorus' references to the stories of Althea, Scylla, and the Lemnian women.

Althea was the wife of Oeneus, King of Calydon. After her son, Meleager, was born, the Fates told her that he would live only as long as a certain log in the fireplace remained unburned. Althea immediately took it, quenched it, and hid it away. Years later Meleager quarreled with his mother's four brothers, and killed them all. The Furies instructed Althea to cast the log on the fire; she did so, and Meleager immediately died. In expiation Althea then hanged herself.

Nisus, King of Megara, had been informed that his kingdom and his life depended on his never cutting a purple lock of hair on his head. His daughter, Scylla (who is not the Scylla of Scylla and Charybdis fame), fell in love with Minos, King of Crete, at the time when he laid siege to Megara. To ingratiate herself with Minos, she cut off her father's lock, thus costing him his life and kingdom. After Minos had sacked the city and was about to sail back to Crete, Scylla, in her passion, swam after his ship and clung to the rudder. At that moment her father's spirit, in the form of an eagle, swooped down on her. In terror she let go and drowned.

The men of Lemnos quarreled with their wives and took Thracian captive women as concubines. Led by Hypsipyle, daughter of Thoas, King of Lemnos, the wives took revenge by slaughtering every man on the island except Thoas; Hypsipyle secretly saved his life by setting him adrift in a boat. When the women of Lemnos later learned of this they sold Hypsipyle into slavery.

None of these stories are gone into in detail by the Chorus, which is a clear indication that Aeschylus assumed they were well known to the Athenians. It is significant that these stories center on the slaying of a child, a parent, and husbands, for the *Oresteia* deals with the killing of a child by Agamemnon, a husband by Clytemnestra, and a parent by Orestes, and the emphasis in all is placed upon the ultimate triumph of Justice in one way or another.

THIRD EPISODE: The setting now shifts to the front of the palace of Clytemnestra and Aegisthus, where it remains for the balance of the drama. Orestes and Pylades appear disguised as travelers and knock on the palace gate. When a servant asks what they desire, they reply hospitality and an opportunity to convey information to the lord and lady of the house. Clytemnestra greets them, asks what they wish, and offers them hot baths and beds for rest; her house has all a weary traveler might desire. Orestes says that Strophius of Phocis had asked him to bear to Argos the news of Orestes' death. Clytemnestra, with some considerable poignancy, laments her son's death, directs that the two travelers be given lodging, and all but the Chorus enter the palace. The Chorus joyfully looks forward to Orestes' revenge, and on seeing Cilissa, his old nurse, come from the palace weeping, they wonder if he has already begun. But she has only been sent by Clytemnestra to bring Aegisthus to hear the news of Orestes' death. The Queen, she says, is affecting sorrow over the news, but inwardly she is overjoyed by it, as will be Aegisthus. Cilissa, however, is truly disconsolate. The Chorus tells her not to obey Clytemnestra's instruction to tell Aegisthus to bring his bodyguard with him, but rather to tell him to come alone. The nurse, wondering what the Chorus might know that she does not, agrees, and goes off to find Aegisthus.

COMMENT: There is a supreme and terrible irony in Clytemnestra's words of welcome to the pretended travelers, for the audience would inevitably recall the welcome she gave Agamemnon. He came home to a bath and his death bed. The house is certainly a haven for weary travelers! There is a further irony in that this time one of the travelers will turn the tables on her.

Because some editors feel that Clytemnestra's laments are out of character, they assign them to Electra. The surviving manuscripts, however, give them specifically to Clytemnestra. This seems sound for at least three reasons. First, Electra would be out of place in this scene. Second, assuming that Orestes and Pylades were really strangers, they would expect this kind of reaction. Third, Clytemnestra's remarks bear a definite resemblance to those she made near the end of *Agamemnon*, when she prayed that the curse on the House of Atreus be at an end, and asserted that she would be content with a small portion of the wealth of the House if such would be the case. Giving her the lines does not make her any more lovable than she would be without them, and assigning them to Electra would add nothing to the depth of her character.

By directing Cilissa to change her message to Aegisthus, the Chorus plays a vital part in the working out of Orestes' vengeance, for if Aegisthus were to come with his bodyguard Orestes' task would be much more difficult, if not impossible. This is one of the very few instances in Greek tragedy where the chorus plays such a vital role.

THIRD STASIMON: The Chorus, in an impassioned prayer, calls upon Zeus and Hermes to protect Orestes and help him in his revenge, and they hope that the curse on the House will then be at an end. And they call upon Orestes not to weaken in his resolve should Clytemnestra beg mercy of her son, but, reminding her of the mercy she showed his father, do the deed he came to do. They also urge him to remember Perseus, and act as he did at his homecoming.

COMMENT: Orestes thus far has shown no indication of indecision, but the Chorus' reference to Perseus is intriguing nonetheless. Perseus was the son of Danae by Zeus. Because Danae's father, Acrisius, had been told by the Delphic oracle that a son of Danae would kill him, he set the two adrift in a chest. They were rescued and cared for by a fisherman of Seriphos. Eventually Polydectes, King of Seriphos, fell in love with Danae and desired to marry her, but he did not want any part of her son. Pretending to be about to marry someone else, Polydectes held a banquet at which wedding gifts were to be given him. Perseus, not having anything, rashly offered to obtain the head of the Gorgon Medusa. Medusa had once been beautiful, but she had once lain with Poseidon in one of Athene's temples and Athene, enraged, had changed her into a winged monster with glaring eyes, huge teeth, protruding tongue, brazen claws, and serpent hair. If anyone looked upon her he was instantly turned to stone.

After many adventures and considerable help from Athene and Hermes, Perseus succeeded in cutting off Medusa's head, which he put in a sack to bring back to Polydectes. Returning to Seriphos Perseus sought his mother but could not find her. He was told that she had refused to marry Polydectes, and his fury had been such that she had been forced to take refuge in a temple. Enraged, Perseus went to the palace where Polydectes was holding a banquet for his friends and companions. As he entered, everyone turned to stare at him in astonishment. He thereupon took the Gorgon's head from his bag and held it aloft. Polydectes and the rest were immediately turned to stone. This is another story not gone into in detail by the Chorus, but which must have been familiar to the audience. The Chorus wants Orestes to be as firm in resolve as Perseus, and, should Clytemnestra ask for mercy, to turn his heart to stone as Perseus turned Polydectes to stone.

FOURTH EPISODE: Aegisthus arrives expressing mixed feelings over the news of Orestes' death. If true, he fears some new penalty will be meted out to the House; but he has doubts that the report is true, for Clytemnestra's hopes and fears might have tricked her. In any case, he himself will question the strangers to make sure. He enters the palace, and almost immediately a loud cry is heard from inside. The Chorus withdraws so as not to interfere or be involved in what is to take place. A Follower of Aegisthus rushes from the palace crying out that Aegisthus has been slain and calling upon Clytemnestra to prepare to defend herself, for she is to be next. She orders him to bring her "an axe to kill a man," and he dashes inside.

Orestes and Pylades come out of the palace with swords drawn; Orestes' is dripping with blood. Clytemnestra asks if "beloved, strong Aegisthus" is indeed dead, and Orestes replies that he is and she shall lie in the same grave with him. She calls upon her son to have pity on her, and bares her breast, reminding him that he had nursed at it when he was a baby. Orestes turns to Pylades and asks if he can possibly be shamed into sparing his mother. Pylades firmly replies that this would violate Apollo's specific and direct command, and Orestes agrees. He tells Clytemnestra he intends to kill her over Aegisthus' body. She continues to plead, asserting that her murder of Agamemnon was fated by the curse on the House of Atreus; Orestes says that his killing of her is part of the working out of the same curse. In response to her statement that a mother also has a curse she can lay upon a son who murders her, he replies that she has not been much of a mother to him; in addition to murdering his father, she virtually sold him into slavery for love of Aegisthus. She denies this, and points to Agamemnon's infidelities while at Troy. In addition, she protests, it is unbearable for a wife to live as a widow while her husband is away. She again threatens Orestes with her curse, but he says that if he fails to kill her he will bring upon himself his father's curse. She recalls her dream and accuses Orestes of being the snake she gave birth to. He agrees, and asserts that as she performed a shameful deed of murder she must and will now receive the penalty, and he forces her into the palace to kill her.

COMMENT: Aegisthus' doubts are quickly resolved; as soon as he enters the palace Orestes kills him. It can now be readily seen how impossible this would have been if he had brought his bodyguard with him. Clytemnestra is immediately aware that she has been duped and she calls for the same axe with which she had cut off Agamemnon's head. Aeschylus does not indicate in *Agamemnon* that Clytemnestra had cut her husband's head off, but it was part of the legend, and in this play there are allusions by both the Chorus and the Follower of Aegisthus that she had indeed done so.

Orestes' question of Pylades is more indicative of rhetoric than of doubt, for he has shown absolutely no hesitation previously, and shows none as this scene proceeds. Pylades answers in three lines, the only lines he speaks in the entire drama. Voiced here, at the climax of the tragedy, they are tremendously effective, for they restate and reemphasize the absolute necessity of Orestes' killing his mother. Note that there are three speaking actors on stage at this point. Though Sophocles added the third actor, this is the earliest surviving play in which he is used.

When Clytemnestra threatens Orestes with her curse, she is referring to the invoking of the Furies. Orestes is forcibly presented with a tragic dilemma: whether he should leave himself open to an inevitable attack by his father's Furies should he fail to kill his mother, or submit to as apparently inevitable an attack by his mother's Furies should he carry out his intention to slay her. He makes the right choice, for if he is to be tormented anyway it is better for his torment to be the result of his taking vengeance than not taking it.

When Orestes accuses her of infidelity, Clytemnestra asserts that she was no more unfaithful than was Agamemnon. This is an obvious attack on the concept of the double standard, but Orestes rejects it, implying that no matter what a husband does his wife's obligation is to remain true and faithful to him.

FOURTH STASIMON: The Chorus returns voicing muted sorrow for the deaths of Clytemnestra and Aegisthus, but Justice came upon them even as it came upon Priam and Troy. Justice came, guided by Apollo and wielded by Orestes, and now may the curse be removed from the House of Atreus, for Agamemnon has been avenged and the kingdom freed of tyranny.

> **COMMENT:**   Though the Chorus throughout the play has looked forward to the slaying of Clytemnestra and Aegisthus, they mourn their deaths because the deaths illustrate the workings of Fate, a curse, crime following crime, and retribution, and the fact that man is constantly caught up by forces which he cannot control. In addition, the death of anyone brings sorrow and the necessity of mourning. Not properly mourning Agamemnon, even though she had murdered him herself, is one of the things the Chorus condemned Clytemnestra for earlier in the play.

EXODOS: The doors of the palace open to reveal Orestes standing over the bodies of Clytemnestra and Aegisthus. Attendants hold the net robe in which Clytemnestra had entangled Agamemnon. He points to the two who first swore together to murder his father, then swore to die together, and have now kept their promise. He orders the net to be displayed so that all can see how right it was for him to kill his mother; Aegisthus' slaying he dismisses, for all know death is the proper punishment for a seducer. He prays that he be spared such a wife as Clytemnestra. Yet, in accomplishing his vengeance, deserved though it was, he has tainted himself: he is now a matricide. Even though Apollo promised him that he would not be doing wrong, nonetheless he will leave Argos as an outcast wanderer. Just as the Chorus tells him his deed was well done and he is the liberator of Argos, he sees the Furies coming to attack him. The Chorus believes he is having hallucinations, but he firmly declares that the coming of the Furies is not a fancy but a fact. He rushes from the stage to seek refuge at Apollo's shrine, as the god had instructed him to do. The Chorus thinks Orestes is going mad, and points to this as the third affliction of the House of Atreus: First, the curse of Thyestes because Atreus had slain his children and served them up to him at a banquet; second, the murder of Agamemnon by his own wife; now, the infliction of madness upon Orestes. They wonder if there will ever be an end, and if so, how?

COMMENT: Orestes and the bodies of Clytemnestra and Aegisthus are revealed in a tableau on the eccyclema, which is wheeled out through the center doors of the skene. All of Orestes' lines in this scene are delivered from there.

The hopes of the Chorus for an end to the curse, expressed in the previous stasimon, are short-lived, as are Orestes' hopes that he might achieve his vengeance unscathed. A crime remains a crime even when it is ordered by a god, and retribution must follow. When, in *The Eumenides*, the Furies appear on stage, it becomes obvious to all that Orestes was not having visions, a fact which gives more meaning and depth to this closing scene than the Chorus realizes.

This scene emphasizes the basic conflict between Apollo, representing Agamemnon and the moral necessity of avenging his foul murder, and the Furies, representing Clytemnestra and the crime against nature of a son killing his mother.

THE EUMENIDES

(458 B.C.)

BACKGROUND: *The Eumenides,* variously translated as *The Kindly Ones* or *The Solemn Ones,* is the third play of the *Oresteia.* It is one of the very few Greek plays in which the Chorus leaves the stage completely and the scene changes entirely. The play begins a few days after the events in *The Libation Bearers.* Although there was a tradition that Orestes had been tried by the Areopagus, most of the action of this drama seems to have been invented by Aeschylus. In fact, there was another tradition that the first trial conducted by the Areopagus was Poseidon's prosecution of Ares for the slaying of Poseidon's son (hence the name Areopagus, or "Ares' Hill").

The Greeks usually tried to avoid using terms or names of actual or seeming ill-omen, substituting instead their opposites or a euphemism. Consequently, the Furies, the Angry Ones or Avenging Ones, became known as the Kindly Ones or the Solemn Ones. Aeschylus asserts in this play, however, that the change of name indicates a real change of character. The Furies were normally, but not always, depicted as punishing murder only when members of the same family were involved, or when a stranger was slain by a host. Normally in cases of murder the kinsmen of the slain person took revenge, but when homicide occurred within a family the kinsmen might naturally refuse to kill one of their own members. Punishment by the blood feud broke down in such cases, and was therefore left to the divine agents.

THEMES: The primary theme of *The Eumenides,* as an individual play, centers on the abandonment of the law requiring a penalty just like the crime (an eye for an eye, a murder for a murder), and the private blood feud in favor of public legal trial. This is symbolized by the conversion of the Furies from Avenging Spirits to Kindly Spirits, and it indicates the adoption

113

of a justice tempered by reason and mercy. The conversion of the Furies, daughters of Erebus (Darkness) and Night, also constitutes a reconciliation of the powers of darkness with the powers of light, or a union of the ancient Fates with Zeus, whose name means "the bright shining light of heaven."

Secondary themes, although at times they tend to dominate the play, deal with patriotic and political concepts. *The Eumenides* was written in Aeschylus' old age, and it was quite obviously intended to constitute a panegyric to Athens, described by him at line 869 as the land most beloved of the gods. He celebrates the divine foundation of the Areopagus, which he describes as the savior of the city and the bulwark of the land. In addition, an alliance had just been negotiated by Athens with Argos. Consequently, although Homer had said that Agamemnon's city was Mycenae, that city had been destroyed by Argos in 468/7 B.C., and by placing the home of Agamemnon at Argos, Aeschylus flatters the Argives as much as he would have insulted them if he had placed it at Mycenae, and thereby makes possible the impressive ratification of eternal friendship between Argos and Athens that occurs in this drama.

CHARACTERS:

PRIESTESS OF APOLLO, THE PYTHIA   Has charge of Apollo's temple at Delphi.

APOLLO   God of the sun and deliverer of oracles. He also brought about the purification of guilt.

GHOST OF CLYTEMNESTRA   Here seeking revenge by the Furies on Orestes, who murdered her.

ORESTES   Son of Agamemnon, former King of Argos, and Clytemnestra.

ATHENE Daughter of Zeus and goddess of the arts, science, wisdom, and power, and protectress of everything that distinguishes civilized society. In particular she was the protectress of Athens.

CHORUS OF EUMENIDES (FURIES) Avenging goddesses who, when the murder of a relative, a breach of hospitality, or perjury was committed, relentlessly pursued the offender and finally drove him mad. Here they appear as women wearing horrible masks.

SECOND CHORUS   Women of Athens.

HERMES

TWELVE JURYMEN
                        } Mute parts.
HERALD

CITIZENS OF ATHENS

SETTING: The first part of the play, to the middle of the second episode, takes place in front of the temple of Apollo at Delphi; the balance at Athens on the Acropolis in front of the temple of Athene. It is possible that the trial is intended to take place on the Areopagus, which was somewhat to the west of the Acropolis.

> **COMMENT:** The precise locality or localities of the second part of the play are deliberately left vague by Aeschylus, partly as a result of the basic informality of background in early Greek tragedy. Also, however, this arrangement allowed the audience to easily visualize a mental shift of scene from Athene's temple to the Areopagus, and such a shift could have been more concretely indicated by a simple change in the painted backdrop hung in front of the skene.

PROLOGUE: The Priestess of Apollo enters and stands before Apollo's temple. She offers prayers to the various divinities who have had an association with the temple: Mother Earth, Themis, Phoebe, Phoebus Apollo, Athene, Poseidon, and Zeus, asking for their aid and guidance since she is about to enter the temple to give oracles. She invites any Hellenes present who might desire prophecies to follow the custom of drawing lots and enter, and goes into the temple. Almost at once she runs out again in great fear and horror. She has seen a man (Orestes), with blood dripping from his hands and holding a bloody sword and an olive branch, crouched at the central altar, and surrounded by horrible, sleeping women (the Furies).

She describes them as Gorgon-like but without wings, black, utterly repulsive, with a poisonous ooze dripping from their eyes and foul breath wheezing from them as they snore. She calls upon Apollo, the cleanser of houses, to come and cleanse his own house.

COMMENT: Delphi was a town on the southern slope of Mt. Parnassus. Apollo slew Python, a serpent that was ravaging the area, and the Delphic sanctuary became the center of the worship of Apollo Pythias (Apollo the Python-killer). Hence the priestess of the temple at Delphi became known as the Pythia, or the Pythian Priestess. Seated on a tripod above a cleft in the ground, from which came overpowering vapors, the Pythia went into a trance and uttered incoherent sounds which were then interpreted by the priests of the temple and given to the pilgrim as his answer.

Mother Earth, or Gaea, was the oldest of the Greek deities. She arose of her own power out of Chaos and produced the sky (Uranus), sea, and mountains. By Uranus she became the mother of the Titans, two of whom, Cronus and Rhea, were the parents of Zeus, Poseidon, Hades, Hera, Demeter, and Hestia. When Cronus attacked his father with a sickle, drops of blood from the wound fell upon Mother Earth, and she gave birth to the Furies. Mother Earth often gave prophecies, originally at Delphi, but later at other places as well.

Thetis was a daughter of Uranus and Gaea. She was the goddess of law and order, and by Zeus was the mother of the Moirae (the Fates) and the Horae (goddesses who represented the order of nature and the changing seasons, and who also protected the moral order). She also gave prophecies at Delphi before the shrine became Apollo's.

The original Phoebe was one of the Titaness daughters of Uranus and Gaea, and was venerated as the goddess of the moon. She also occupied the oracle of Delphi before Apollo. Later Artemis, twin sister of Apollo, whose parents were Zeus and Leto, became the goddess of the moon (as well as of the hunt) by virtue of her association with her brother, who was god of the sun. Aeschylus has here combined the attributes of Phoebe and Artemis.

Phoebus Apollo (Phoebus is the masculine form of Phoebe) was the son of Zeus and Leto, and the twin brother of Artemis. He was the god of the sun, goodness, beauty, and harmonious peace, the preserver of law and order, the purifier of the guilt-ridden conscience, and the deliverer of oracles, particularly at Delphi.

Athene was the daughter of Zeus and Metis. Zeus swallowed Metis, fearing that her child would surpass him in power and usurp his throne, and Athene sprang from his head, fully grown and armed. She was the goddess of wisdom, the arts, sciences, and womanly crafts, and the protectress of civilized society, in which role she maintained justice and law and had the people's assembly, the Areopagus, meet under her protection. She was also venerated as the goddess of war. Athens was under her special protection.

Poseidon was a son of Cronus and Rhea, and brother of Zeus and Hades. When the universe was divided up Zeus received the sky and earth, Hades the underworld, and Poseidon all waters. Consequently, he was god of the sea and water. He had no apparent connection with Delphi, but *The Eumenides* was written for an Athenian audience who, as inhabitants of a state which achieved its grandeur through its fleet, would expect to have him included in a list of specially venerated divinities.

Zeus was the supreme god of the Greeks, the father of gods and mankind, and the lord of the universe. He was the god of counsel, the protector of the people's assembly, and the preserver of the oath. The family was also under his care, as were guests and strangers. He oversaw the harmony not only of nature but also of the social order, and under this latter attribute was the protector and bringer of justice. He, too, gave many oracles, often through his favorite son, Apollo.

An awareness of the attributes and relevance of the deities

named by the Priestess was assumed by Aeschylus, and is essential to an adequate appreciation of the play. Orestes' case is to be generalized into a struggle between the old gods and the new gods, especially Apollo (light), Athene (wisdom), and Zeus (justice), and the old and new conceptions of justice. The old justice was based on the premise that the perpetrator must suffer punishment equal to his crime, and therefore one crime led to further crimes and the blood feud, which often involved the innocent along with the guilty. The new justice was also based on the concept that the criminal must be punished, but that justice must be tempered by reason and mercy. Consequently, the state would take over the role of the dispenser of justice, and blood feuds would be unnecessary, and Athens, through this reconciliation of opposing forces, would become a harmonious, righteous, happy, blessed, and powerful city. A corollary of this, that the female (Clytemnestra) must be subordinated to the male (Orestes, Agamemnon), is also urged by Aeschylus in the play.

FIRST EPISODE: The doors of the temple open to show Orestes clinging to the central altar and surrounded by the sleeping Furies. Apollo and Hermes are standing beside him. Apollo speaks to Orestes and promises never to forsake him. He points to the Furies, whom he has temporarily lulled to sleep with his craft. They are, he says, creatures loathed by both men and gods, who because of this dwell in Tartarus. He will not be able to keep them inactive permanently, however, and for this reason he tells Orestes to take refuge at Athene's temple in Athens, where he is to kneel and embrace her statue. Then will come those who will judge him and free him of the afflictions of the Furies. Apollo knows this will happen, for he himself ordered Orestes to slay his mother. Apollo then directs Hermes to guide Orestes to Athens, and the three leave. The Ghost of Clytemnestra enters and rebukes the Furies for sleeping and letting Orestes escape. She reminds them of the many prayers and libations she offered them, often in preference to the other gods, while she was alive, and yet they refuse to bring her vengeance upon Orestes, who even now is laughing at them. She shows the gashes he inflicted, and mentions her own name. The Furies begin to stir and mutter in their sleep. Clytemnestra continues to berate them, and they begin to dream they are pursuing Orestes. Clytemnestra upbraids them, telling them to stop pursuing her son in their dreams and pursue him in fact, and wither and shrivel him. The Ghost disappears as the Furies waken.

> **COMMENT:** There is some debate as to how Orestes, Apollo, Hermes, and the Chorus of Furies were revealed to the audience, but it is most probable that they were on the eccyclema, which was wheeled out through the center doors of the skene. Tartarus was the most terrible section of the Underworld. It was a bottomless pit under the earth where Zeus shut up the Titans and a number of monsters. Hermes was a half-brother of Apollo. Zeus was the father of both, but Leto was Apollo's mother, while Maia was the mother of Hermes. Hermes is depicted here in his attribute as messenger of the gods.
>
> These opening scenes are extremely gory in appearance. Orestes is shown with blood on his hands and sword, and the Ghost of Clytemnestra displays her bloody wounds, all of which help to emphasize the horror of Orestes' deed. It should be noted that it is not until the Ghost mentions Clytemnestra's name that the Furies are aroused. Apollo's craft has been sufficient to lull them temporarily, as he said, but the name of the one seeking vengeance is more powerful.

PARODOS: The Chorus of Furies bemoans their being duped by Apollo, thereby allowing Orestes to escape. They accuse Apollo of robbing them, and complain that he and the other younger gods flout the elder gods and their laws. Because of this Apollo has defiled his own temple and the center-stone of the earth. Nevertheless, he will not succeed in his attempt to have Orestes escape, for they will pursue him, and one of his descendants shall yet kill him.

> **COMMENT:** The Furies make it obvious that a tremendous clash is going to take place between the elder gods, represented by themselves, and the younger ones, represented primarily by Apollo and later Athene. Ancient prerogatives, the conception of justice, and the manner of maintaining it among mankind are at stake. These subjects eventually overshadow the personal fate of Orestes as the

drama proceeds. The center-stone was known as the Om-
phalos. It was a sacred stone considered to be the center
of the world, and was kept at the temple of Apollo. The
Furies' closing lines make further reference to both the
traditional concept of a crime for a crime and the expected continuance of the curse on the House of Atreus.

SECOND EPISODE: Apollo comes from the inner sanctuary
and orders the Furies to leave his temple. They should not be
polluting an oracular shrine, but should rather be where heads
are being cut off, eyes gouged out, throats cut, and other muti-
lations occurring, for such are their proper places, and this
makes them detested by all the other gods. They reply that the
responsibility for their being in his temple is his, for he was the
one who ordered Orestes to kill his mother. Therefore the guilt,
as well, is his. He asks how he is guilty, and they answer that
he urged on a matricide and then gave him shelter, and it is
their function to pursue matricides. Apollo asks what about
wives who kill their husbands? They say that this would not
involve the shedding of kindred blood, and therefore they
would not be concerned. Apollo asserts that this position is inconsistent, and, further, it demeans both Hera and Aphrodite.
He says he shall appeal Orestes' case to Athene. No matter,
reply the Furies, they will continue to hunt Orestes, and Apollo
repeats that he will continue to protect him. The Chorus and
Apollo now leave the stage.

The scene changes to the Acropolis, in Athens. The statue of
Athene is in the foreground, her temple in the background. Orestes enters and supplicatingly embraces the foot of the statue.

Orestes prays to Athene, saying he is there at Apollo's orders.
He is no longer a completely unwashed criminal, he claims, for
he has been purified during the wanderings he undertook, also
at Apollo's behest. He awaits the outcome of his trial. The
Chorus of Furies enters, searching for Orestes. They liken
themselves to hunting hounds following the trail of a wounded
fawn, for they have been following the trail of the blood crime
committed by Orestes. Suddenly they spy him, and cry out that
he cannot escape the penalty of blood for blood, that they
themselves are going to suck him dry of blood to repay him for
spilling his mother's blood on the ground. Then they will drag
him to the Underworld, where Hades has already noted his

crime. Orestes protests that when he was a suppliant at Apollo's temple he was unclean, but that having obeyed the god's instructions he has expiated his deed, and he calls upon Athene to free him from the hounding of the Furies. But they declare that neither Apollo nor Athene can save him; they, the Furies, will inevitably feed on him.

> **COMMENT:** The argument over blood relationship versus non-blood relationship makes it obvious that much of the ensuing trial will be based upon technicalities and their interpretation. In fact, much of the trial will hinge on quibbles such as this. Apollo invokes Hera, a daughter of Cronus and Rhea and sister-wife of Zeus, in her attribute as the guardian goddess of marriage, and Aphrodite, daughter of Zeus by Dione, in her attribute as goddess of love, particularly marital love, to indicate that the case is not as simple as the Furies claim it is. They maintain Hera and Aphrodite have nothing to do with the problem, but the point is that the sanctity of marriage is at least as important as the sanctity of the family, and for either side to win completely would be intolerable to the other. Aeschylus is saying, therefore, that Orestes' penalty must of necessity be mitigated.

As indicated in the Background to this play, this is one of the few Greek dramas in which the Chorus leaves the stage entirely. This departure is structurally necessary since the scene changes so drastically from Delphi to Athens. Also, it allows Orestes to appear on stage, at Athene's temple, alone, and then permits the Furies to reappear in search of him. The amount of time that elapses between Orestes' departure from Delphi and his arrival at Athens is left indefinite by Aeschylus, but according to the legend it was a year. For further discussion of this point, see the chapter on the *Oresteia*.

In *The Libation Bearers*, Clytemnestra referred to the Furies as hounds (of Hell, or Hades), and said that they would hound Orestes if he killed her. The reference by the Furies to themselves as hunting hounds is, therefore, readily understandable. Hunting hounds are trained to follow a fresh blood scent, and while the physical blood on Orestes has presumably dried by now (though when this play opens, a few days after the events in *The Libation Bearers*, he is described as still dripping Clytemnestra's blood), the aroma of the crime itself still remains.

FIRST STASIMON: The Furies maintain that they are pursuing their proper function, and that no man whose hands are not defiled by a blood crime committed within his family need fear them. They call upon the Darkness that gave birth to them to bear witness that this is so, and that Apollo is attempting to keep them from what is theirs, namely, Orestes. When the God of Blood causes a man to slay one of his kindred, they will torment that man not only in life but also after death; there can be no escape, not even through the interference of other gods. Even the robes they wear, black instead of white, are proof they are to be avengers and pursuers. Men, in their pride, think they can commit crimes with impunity, but they are wrong; there is no escape from the punishment inflicted by the Furies. They, the Avengers, despised even by the gods, and driven by them from the light into the darkness, nevertheless maintain their sway over mankind, and all men fear them, for their power is primeval.

COMMENT: The Furies were the daughters of Mother Earth (see the Comment to the Prologue). But Cronus attacked his father, Uranus, at night while he slept. Consequently, the Furies, having been born at night as the result of a blood crime committed at night, are, metaphorically, daughters of night and darkness. Their function of tormenting the perpetrator of a blood crime against a member of his family derives from their having been born as the result of such a crime. Their references to their black robes and their having been cast out of the light into the darkness reinforces the idea of them as powers of darkness, and their statement that their power is primeval again emphasizes the struggle that is going to take place between the ancient gods and concepts and the new ones.

The God of Blood is Ares, son of Zeus and Hera, god of war and bloodshed. Because of his cruelty and aggressiveness he was detested by all the gods, including his father.

THIRD EPISODE: Athene enters, dressed in her armor and carrying the aegis. She had, she says, been at Troy to take possession of land promised her by the Greeks. She came because she heard the contention at her shrine. She sees the Furies, asks who the horrible creatures are, and then apologizes for her unkind words, for hers is a temple of justice and honor where evil is not even to be spoken. The Furies identify themselves, and state that they are pursuing Orestes because he murdered his mother. Athene asks why the crime was committed, and the Furies say that the reason is irrelevant, it is the deed only that matters. Athene accuses them of wanting to act righteously but not rightly, and the Furies invite her to judge the case herself.

She turns to Orestes and asks where he comes from, what is his lineage, what he has done, and why he is at her shrine as a supplicant in the tradition of Ixion. He replies that he is not a supplicant bearing a blood-guilt, for he has long since offered the sacrifices required to cleanse himself. As for the rest, he is from Argos and he is the son of Agamemnon. He recounts the story of the murder of his father and the vengeance he himself took upon his mother, and asks Athene to decide whether he was right or wrong. The goddess states that Orestes' case is not only too great a matter to be decided by any mortal man, but that not even she herself can decide it. As one who has been cleansed, Orestes has the right to freedom; yet because he admits killing his mother, the Furies have the right to pursue him, and she can not rule in favor of one without violating the rights of the other. Therefore, she says, she will create a court, to last for all time, and appoint as judges the best Athenian citizens. They will hear the case and render a true judgment.

COMMENT: Athene probably enters via the mechane. She appears in her martial aspect to symbolize her power and authority. She therefore is wearing her helmet and carrying her shield, lance, and aegis. The aegis originally belonged to Zeus, but he turned it over to his warrior daughter. It was a kind of cloak made of goatskin, fringed with serpents covered with scales, and with the Gorgon's head in the center. When shaken, the aegis caused thunder and lightning, and brought fear and terror to the hearts of enemies. Athene was promised certain territory in return for her aid to the Greeks during the Trojan War, and now that the war is over she has been off settling her claims. However, no distance is so great that she cannot hear the dispute taking place at her chief shrine.

Athene's statement to the Furies that they are concerned with acting righteously but not rightly is her way of saying that they are interested merely in the formality but not the essence of justice. In other words, if there are mitigating circumstances to a crime, then the punishment, too, must be mitigated; justice must be tempered with mercy.

Her reference to Ixion is interesting, and somewhat ironic. Ixion was the King of the Lapithae. After murdering his father-in-law he appealed to Athene and was purified and admitted by Zeus to the table of the gods. He thereupon violated his host's hospitality by attempting to seduce Hera, Zeus' wife. Zeus caught him and hurled him into Tartarus, where he was tied to a fiery wheel which revolved perpetually over a fiery pit.

The fact that while Orestes freely admits being a matricide he has also performed the ritual sacrifices required for the purification of the perpetrator of a blood crime creates the dilemma in which Athene finds herself. If she were to judge in favor of the Furies she would deny the validity of Orestes' purification; if she were to judge in his favor she would deny the right of the Furies to pursue a matricide. Aeschylus has her neatly sidestep the dilemma by convening a court of Athenian citizens. The plural is important, for she has already said that one mortal alone would not be qualified to judge the case. Twelve, which is the number she returns with later, acting in concert, presumably would be so qualified. This is Aeschylus' way of saying that the Areopagus is to be the highest tribunal of the affairs of mankind, superseding even the judgment of the gods. That the court is to last for all time is a further indication of Aeschylus' patriotism: he could foresee no end to the greatness and institutions of the Athenian state.

SECOND STASIMON: The Furies complain that the old laws are about to be overthrown. Fear alone, they say, fear of equal retribution prevents man from committing crimes. Remove that fear and crime will be rampant, no one shall be safe: parent, child, neighbor, guest. License will reign supreme. Orestes, therefore, must not be acquitted.

COMMENT: It is obvious that Aeschylus presents both Athene and the Furies as being desirous of preventing crime, especially murder. It is also obvious that all agree that a criminal should be punished. But the murder of Clytemnestra was not punishable in the normal way, thus proving that the normal way is inadequate. Therefore a new way, the institution of a civil court, is necessary to insure that *all* crimes can be punished, and that extenuating circumstances, as in Orestes' case, can be taken into consideration when the punishment is handed down. The new way, consequently, is actually to be more just than the old way.

FOURTH EPISODE: Athene re-enters, with twelve Athenian citizens. She is accompanied by a herald, and followed by a crowd of other Athenians. The scene has presumably changed to the Areopagus. She calls upon the herald to announce the establishment of the court so that the people can assemble there and hear the case. Apollo enters, and states that he will testify on Orestes' behalf, in addition to acting, in effect, as his defense counsel, since it was he who ordered Orestes to kill Clytemnestra. Athene declares the trial open, and directs the Furies to present their side of the case, since they are the prosecutors. They proceed to question Orestes, and he confesses to having killed his mother. He did it, he says, by cutting her throat. Further, he was instructed by Apollo to kill her. His further justification is that she murdered her husband, his father, and the Furies did not descend to punish her for that crime. They say that Agamemnon was not Clytemnestra's blood-relation, and Orestes asks if, indeed, he was. The Furies say he was.

Orestes turns his defense over to Apollo, who states that he followed Zeus' will in instructing Orestes to kill his mother. He cites the baseness of Agamemnon's death: he, the most outstanding Greek leader, murdered by a treacherous and deceitful woman. Apollo reviles the Furies, and argues that Orestes was not a blood-relation of Clytemnestra. The woman merely nourishes the man's seed; therefore only the father is blood-kin to the child. He offers as proof Athene herself, who was born from her father's head, and did not even need her mother's womb to nourish her. In conclusion he tells Athene (and the jurors) that he will make her city, Athens, and its people great, and that Orestes will be loyal to her forever, if she will judge in his favor.

Athene declares the arguments ended, and calls upon the jury to render its decision. She urges them to judge wisely and without fear, for if they do so the court will endure and no man need fear injustice. If they do not, there will be anarchy. She and Apollo remind the jurors of the oaths they swore to give true judgment, and the twelve come forward, one by one, to drop their ballots in the urn at the front of the stage. While they cast their votes, Apollo and the Furies threaten them with reprisals should they vote against their respective sides. The Furies assert that if Apollo wins it will be because he used trickery, just as he had in the case of Admetus, but he replies that it would be wrong for a god to refuse to aid a supplicant who offers him sacrifices and implores his help. Athene says that in case of a tie, she will vote for Orestes, justifying her action on the grounds that she was not, indeed, born of her mother, and that as goddess of war she is male-like in feeling. The ballots are counted and the result is a tie. Athene thereupon declares that Orestes is acquitted. Orestes declares the eternal fealty of himself and Argos to Athene and Athens, and he and Apollo leave.

> **COMMENT:** The trial of Orestes is similar in many respects to the actual trials that took place before the Areopagus, and many of these practices are still followed in courts of the Western world. There is a pre-trial examination, or hearing, the prosecution speaks first and the accused last, the jurors are reminded of their oaths and exhorted to give a just verdict, and in the case of a tie the accused is acquitted. In addition, Apollo appears as an "expert" witness to testify that a mother is not a blood-relation of a child, an argument used also by Sophocles, in *Electra*, and Euripides, in *Orestes*, and presents an example in the form of Athene, he offers a bribe to both Athene and the jurors, and both he and the Furies threaten the judges as they cast their ballots. Considering all these factors, it would seem to be a matter of amazement if any just verdicts were ever rendered by the Areopagus, but the amazing fact is that the unjust verdict was the distinct exception.
>
> The jurors are, of course, all men, for only men could be citizens. Refer to Chapter 1 for a further discussion of Greek citizenship.

Since this play was written by Aeschylus to glorify, among other things, the court of the Areopagus, he naturally has taken great pains in this scene (as well as in preceding scenes) to present its divine origin: the patron goddess of the city herself instituted it.

Orestes states that he killed Clytemnestra by cutting her throat, but in the First Episode Clytemnestra bared her heart and pointed to the wounds he had inflicted. This is not necessarily inconsistent, for even if Orestes had only cut her throat, the mere fact that a son killed his mother would figuratively wound the mother's heart as well.

Admetus was the King of Pherae. Apollo promised him the gift of eternal life if, when it came time for him to die, a member of his family would voluntarily consent to die for him. When his time came, Apollo gained him a short reprieve by making the Three Fates drunk, thereby preventing the cutting of his life's thread. Admetus begged each of his aged parents to die in his stead, and they refused. Alcestis, his wife, learning of the terms of the agreement, took poison, thereby completing the thwarting of the Fates.

As mentioned in the Themes section, Argos and Athens had entered into an alliance shortly before the play was written. Consequently, Aeschylus has Orestes, after his acquittal, promise the eternal loyalty of his city, Argos, to Athens. This is another example of Aeschylus' patriotism and political loyalty.

THIRD STASIMON: The Furies complain that the younger gods have overthrown the laws of the other gods, and that in retribution they shall bring plague, pestilence, destruction, death, and desolation to Athens.

COMMENT: This extremely short Stasimon allows for a brief transition from the departure of Orestes and Apollo to the conversion of the Furies from Avenging Ones to Kindly Ones. It also indicates what the Athenians had to look forward to if that conversion had not taken place.

EXODOS: Athene argues that the Furies have not really been disgraced, that Orestes' acquittal was the will of Zeus. She appeals to them not to fulfill their threats, offers them an underground home at Athens, a home that shall be theirs forever, and promises that the Athenians will give them perpetual devotion. They remain adamant, and Athene, after threatening them with Zeus' thunderbolts, repeats her offer. In a continuing exchange, Athene flatters the Furies, and tells them they will never be as happy anywhere else as they can be at Athens, the country beloved of the gods. She promises that if they stay they may prevent any household that does not honor them from prospering. Relenting, the Furies agree, and they and Athene foretell the glory and happiness that Athens is to know. The Furies then assume benevolent functions, and are renamed the Eumenides (Kindly Ones) by Athene, who leads them in a procession to their new home. The Second Chorus, made up of Athenian women, joins the procession, praises the Eumenides, promises the fealty of Athens to them, and calls upon Zeus to confirm the compact.

> **COMMENT:** Since Orestes left the play at the conclusion of the Fourth Episode, it now becomes quite obvious that the main themes of the play center upon the glorification of the Areopagus as a tribunal dispensing man-made justice as opposed to the god-made justice of the Furies, and of Athens itself. For a further discussion of these points, refer to the Themes section.
>
> The thunderbolt was a gift given to Zeus by the Cyclopes, three wild, one-eyed giants who were sons of Uranus and Mother Earth. (Not the same Cyclops that Odysseus encountered in his travels.) Zeus first used it to strike down his father, Cronus. Subsequently he used it to punish any wrongdoer, including gods, and occasionally he lent it to Athene.
>
> As indicated in the chapter on the *Oresteia*, it was Orestes who, in the original legend of the House of Atreus, first called the Furies the Kindly Ones. Aeschylus is dramatically justified in making Athene the first one to use the expression, however, for by the time she does so, not only has Orestes been acquitted, but the Furies have promised glory, prosperity, and happiness to Athens, thereby indicating that they have completed their transformation. At the conclusion of the trial they had not changed at all.

ESSAY QUESTIONS AND ANSWERS

1. What are some of the major ways in which Aeschylus' plays reflect Athenian social beliefs?

ANSWER: The Athenians achieved a union of civilized life and political liberty, and believed that service and responsibility to the polis, or city-state, was of utmost importance to the making of a good citizen. On the other hand, they also believed that it was the responsibility of the polis to provide for its citizens the scope for the realization of the good life. But people cannot be free under tyranny; therefore, tyranny is wrong. In five of his plays Aeschylus presents tyrants or incipient tyrants. In *The Suppliant Women* there is Aegyptus; in *The Persians* there is Xerxes; in *Prometheus Bound* there is Zeus; in *Agamemnon* and *The Libation Bearers* there are Clytemnestra and Aegisthus. Every one is presented as evil, and every one is defeated. King Pelasgus, in *The Suppliant Maidens*, and Prometheus, in *Prometheus Bound*, are presented as noble characters because they defied tyranny and helped people achieve a better life. In Athenian society the men were predominant, the women subordinated. In the *Oresteia*, Aeschylus presents a reversal of that situation; Clytemnestra ruled Argos during the absence of her husband, Agamemnon, and after she murdered him upon his return from Troy she continued to rule. However, her rule is condemned by every character in the first two plays except herself, and when Orestes is being tried, in *The Eumenides*, for killing her, part of his defense hinges on the assertion, which is accepted by the jury, that his murder of her was of less consequence than her murder of Agamemnon. The Athenians also felt a great loyalty and patriotism toward Athens, and believed that every Greek should feel the same way toward his own city. Consequently, it was evil to betray or attack your city. This belief constitutes one of the themes of *Seven Against Thebes,* and Polyneices, who instigates an attack on his native city of Thebes, is killed in the course of it. An example of Aeschylus' personal patriotism and loyalty to Athens is contained in *The Eumenides,* which is largely concerned with the founding of the Athenian court of the Areopagus, the highest Athenian court of justice.

2. What did the Greeks mean by *sôphrosynê* and *hubris*?

ANSWER: *Sôphrosynê,* in essence, meant moderation. In practical terms this meant obedience to law and self-restraint, especially in the face of any temptation to subordinate civic loyalty to personal ambition or to abuse wealth or power. It also implied the ability of a person or community to act with a balanced judgment at any critical moment. *Hubris* was the opposite of sôphrosynê. It meant the violent overstepping of the mark, the insolence of wealth or triumph, the pride of life and self that trampled underfoot the unwritten law of gods and men. Hubris was the nearest Greek equivalent for sin.

3. What was a *tetralogy*?

ANSWER: A *tetralogy* was a single presentation by one tragic poet. It consisted of three tragedies, originally on different subjects, but eventually on different aspects of the same subject and theme, known as a trilogy (toward the end of the fifth century B.C. the trilogy again contained plays on separate subjects or themes), and one satyr-play, which usually included Dionysus among its characters.

4. What are the major parts or sections of a tragedy?

ANSWER: A tragedy has five major parts: *prologue, parodos, episode, stasimon,* and *exodos.* The *prologue* is an introductory scene in which the protagonist gives his opening speech. The *prologue* is followed by the *parodos,* which is the opening song of the chorus. An *episode* is a dramatic scene involving one or more actors and, usually, the chorus. Episodes are separated from each other by *stasimons,* odes sung or chanted by the chorus. The *exodos* is the concluding scene and song of the chorus.

5. What were the major parts of a Greek theatre?

ANSWER: The major parts of a Greek theatre were the *orchestra*, a circular area where the chorus and actors performed; the *skene*, a building at the back of the orchestra where actors changed and costumes and props were stored, and in front of which the plays were performed; the *proscenium*, a decorative facade built in front of the skene; the *parascenium*, a wing projecting toward the orchestra added to either side of the proscenium. On either side of the skene there was a *parodos*, or entrance, by which the spectators entered the theatre and the chorus entered the stage, or orchestra.

6. What are the main themes presented by Aeschylus in his tragedies?

ANSWER: Of the many themes in Aeschylus' extant dramas, the ones that recur most often involve the triumph of justice over violence and brute force, the necessity of personal responsibility for one's actions, the possibility of complete retribution for sin, the inevitability of punishment of pride, self-will and sacrilege, the belief that man has basic inherent limitations, and the concept that life is essentially tragic but that it is possible to acquire wisdom through suffering.

7. How does King Pelasgus, in *The Suppliant Maidens*, reflect the Greek concept of hospitality?

ANSWER: Hospitality was an obligation. If a stranger knocked on the door he was to be invited in and treated like a guest. Any discourtesy or ill-will shown him was a violation of hospitality, and was considered to be evil. Zeus himself was the protector of hospitality, which in itself indicates the high regard in which the concept was held. King Pelasgus is presented with a dilemma: should he grant sanctuary to the Danaids, thus incurring the wrath of Aegyptus, or should he refuse, thus insuring that the Danaids will commit suicide in the sacred grove of his city? He places the concept of hospitality above the potential safety of himself and his city, fully confident that Zeus will support both in the end.

8. What are some of the ways in which *The Persians* is a unique Greek drama?

ANSWER: *The Persians* is the only surviving Greek play that deals with an historical subject. Although it is concerned with the Greek victory over the despotic Persians at Salamis, the Persians are presented sympathetically and with great nobility. Finally, though this play glorifies a great Greek victory, its action takes place at the Persian capital, and not one Greek hero is named.

9. Why is *Seven Against Thebes* generally considered to be more epic in structure than dramatic?

ANSWER: The Second Episode, which comes precisely in the middle of the play, and occupies almost precisely one-third of it, is a static scene in which the seven Argive champions are enumerated and minutely described by the Messenger. The same is also done for the Theban heroes by Eteocles. This kind of enumeration, which occupies a major portion of both the *Iliad* and the *Odyssey*, is essentially epic in nature rather than dramatic.

10. What seem to be the major themes of *Prometheus Bound*, and why is it difficult to be certain about them?

ANSWER: *Prometheus Bound* is considered to be the first play of a trilogy of which the second and third plays are now lost. Any attempt at interpretation is therefore risky. However, the basic themes seem to involve the conflict and ultimate reconciliation between tyranny and brute force, represented by Zeus, and justice and intelligence, represented by Prometheus. Other themes seem to center on the problems of the ultimate nature of the divine power that controls the universe and why there are evil and suffering in the world.

11. What is unusual about the staging of *Prometheus Bound*?

ANSWER: Virtually all of the action takes place on a rocky cliff or crag which was probably higher than the skene. This is necessitated by the fact that Prometheus is chained to the cliff. Almost all of the characters: Prometheus, Might, Violence, Hephaestus, Oceanus, and the Chorus of Oceanids, are on either the cliff or the mechane throughout the entire play. Io is the only one to perform in the more usual place, the orchestra.

12. What are the overall themes of the *Oresteia*?

ANSWER: The primary theme centers on an inherited blood feud and the necessity of its final replacement by public legal process. Aeschylus rejects the earlier Greek idea that members of families had to inflict a blood revenge for a blood crime and that therefore murder must follow murder in an unending chain. Other themes are that the doer of an evil deed must suffer punishment; suffering of one kind or another is inevitable but from suffering comes wisdom; and that too much worldly success leads to the sin of hubris, which in turn leads to eventual ruin and destruction.

13. Why does Clytemnestra murder Agamemnon?

ANSWER: Clytemnestra specifies two reasons for murdering her husband. First, he sacrificed their daughter, Iphigenia, in order to obtain favorable winds for his fleet on the way to Troy. Thus he put the prospects of the conquest of Troy and his becoming a great leader and hero ahead of the safety and well-being of his family. Second, he has brought back from Troy King Priam's daughter, Cassandra, to be his mistress. Thus he is slighting Clytemnestra and her position as his wife. But there is a third reason, which Clytemnestra does not mention. During Agamemnon's absence she has taken Aegisthus as her lover, and she herself has ruled the kingdom for ten years. She desires neither to lose her power nor to have her infidelity revealed to her husband.

14. What attitudes toward the Trojan War are expressed in *Agamemnon*?

ANSWER: There are both positive and negative attitudes expressed. The Watchman condemns the war because during Agamemnon's ten-year absence evils have come to Argos: Clytemnestra has become a tyrant and has betrayed her husband by taking a lover. Clytemnestra herself condemns the war because it caused the death of her daughter, Iphigenia. It is the Chorus that is most outspoken in its hatred of the war, however, for many Greeks, and Trojans as well, have been killed and many homes in Argos are now permanently bereft of their men, all because of a woman: Helen. These terrible things are not worth the getting back of a woman for her husband, even if that husband is Menelaus. But a quite different attitude is held by Agamemnon, who looked upon the war as an opportunity to gain renown, and is satisfied.

15. What is the theme of *The Libation Bearers*?

ANSWER: The theme is the revenge of Orestes upon Clytemnestra and Aegisthus for the murder of Agamemnon. As in *Agamemnon* the emphasis is on Clytemnestra's professed reasons for killing her husband: the sacrifice of Iphigenia and the bringing back of Cassandra, so here too the emphasis is on Orestes professed reasons for killing his mother: her slaying of his father and her infidelity. There has therefore been a slight shifting of emphasis, for Clytemnestra's infidelity was only alluded to in *Agamemnon*. Aeschylus is here presenting the basic irreconcilability of blood revenge with outside legal justice, and the necessity of the latter to be paramount.

16. What are the two techniques that are first used in this play?

ANSWER: This is the first extant play to contain a recognition scene (in which Electra recognizes, by the presence of a lock of his hair and his footprints, that her brother Orestes has been at their father's tomb), and an intrigue (in which Orestes reveals to the Chorus how he plans to kill Aegisthus and Clytemnestra).

17. What is the major theme of *The Eumenides*?

ANSWER: The major theme involves the rejection of the older law of inflicting on the perpetrator of a crime a punishment exactly equivalent to the crime, and consequently of the blood feud, in favor of public legal trial. The corollary of this is the celebration, by Aeschylus, of the founding of the Areopagus, the supreme court of Athens.

18. In what ways is the trial of Orestes similar to trials that actually took place before the Areopagus?

ANSWER: There is a pre-trial hearing; the prosecution speaks first and the accused last; before rendering their verdict the jurors, who are all men, are reminded of the oaths they swore to decide justly; in the event of a tie vote the accused is acquitted; there is an "expert" witness; and bribes and threats are offered to the jurors.

BIBLIOGRAPHY AND GUIDE TO FURTHER RESEARCH

AESCHYLUS: PLAYS

Campbell, Lewis. *Aeschylus: The Seven Plays*. Oxford: Oxford University Press (The World's Classics).

Corrigan, Robert W. *Masterpieces of Classical Drama*. (Contains *Agamemnon, The Libation Bearers, The Eumenides,* and *Prometheus Bound*.) New York: Dell Publishing Company. (paperback, 60¢)

Grene, David, and Richmond Lattimore. *The Complete Greek Tragedies,* vol. I. Chicago: University of Chicago Press. Also, Chicago: University of Chicago Press (Phoenix Books). (paperback, 1.50)

Oates, Whitney J., and Eugene O'Neill, Jr. *The Complete Greek Drama*, vol. I. New York: Random House.

Roche, Paul. *The Orestes Plays of Aeschylus*. New York: New American Library of World Literature (Mentor Books). (paperback, 75¢)

————. *Prometheus Bound*. New York: New American Library of World Literature (Mentor Books). (paperback, 60¢)

Smyth, Herbert Weir. *Aeschylus*. 2 vols. Loeb Classical Library. Cambridge, Massachusetts: Harvard University Press.

Vellacott, Philip. *The Oresteian Trilogy*. Baltimore, Maryland: Penguin Books. (paperback, 95¢)

————. *Prometheus and Other Plays*. (*The Suppliant Maidens, The Persians, Seven Against Thebes.*) Baltimore, Maryland: Penguin Books. (paperback, 95¢)

AESCHYLUS: CRITICISM

Murray, Gilbert. *Aeschylus: The Creator of Tragedy*. Oxford: Oxford University Press. An incisive and stimulating discussion of Aeschylus and his plays.

Sheppard, John T. *Aeschylus and Sophocles: Their Work and Influence*. New York: Longmans, Green and Company (Our Debt to Greece and Rome). An excellent comparative analysis of the two tragic poets.

Smyth, Herbert Weir. *Aeschylean Tragedy*. Berkeley, California: University of California Press. An excellent presentation of Aeschylus' approach to tragedy.

FIFTH CENTURY GREECE

Agard, Walter R. *The Greek Mind*. Princeton, New Jersey: Princeton University Press. Also, New York: D. Van Nostrand and Company (Anvil Books). (paperback, 1.45) A good general discussion.

Bowra, C. M. *The Greek Experience*. New York: The World Publishing Company. Also, New York: New American Library of World Literature (Mentor Books). (paperback, 60¢) A standard work on Greece.

Cambridge Ancient History, vol. V. Cambridge: Cambridge University Press. An outstanding work, with sometimes excessive detail.

Encyclopedia of the Classical World. Englewood Cliffs, New Jersey: Prentice-Hall, Inc. (paperback, 2.95) A ready-reference guide to people, places, and institutions.

Hamilton, Edith. *The Greek Way to Western Civilization*. Boston: Little, Brown and Company. Also, New York: New American Library of World Literature (Mentor Books). (paperback, 60¢) A solid introduction to Greek thought and society.

Kitto, Humphrey D. F. *The Greeks*. Harmondsworth: Penguin Books. (paperback, 95¢) A fine presentation of fifth century Greek ideas and social developments.

MYTHOLOGY

Blakeney, E, H., ed. *Smith's Smaller Classical Dictionary*. New York: E. P. Dutton and Company. Brief articles on most Greek myths and mythological characters.

Encyclopedia of Classical Mythology. Englewood Cliffs, New Jersey: Prentice-Hall, Inc. (paperback, 2.45) A ready reference guide to classical myth and legend.

Graves, Robert. *The Greek Myths*. 2 vols. Baltimore, Maryland: Penguin Books. (paperback, 1.45 each) The most comprehensive presentation of the Greek myths.

Harvey, Sir Paul. *The Oxford Companion to Classical Literature*. Oxford: Oxford University Press. A comprehensive, but often too brief presentation of the myths and the works in which they are found.

GENERAL WORKS ON THE GREEK THEATRE AND DRAMA

Bieber, Margarete. *The History of the Greek and Roman Theater*. Princeton, New Jersey: Princeton University Press. Contains 566 excellent illustrations and a brief, rather thin text.

Flickinger, Roy C. *The Greek Theater and Its Drama*. Chicago: University of Chicago Press. Still an outstanding work, with a fine section on Aeschylus, though in need of revision.

Goodell, Thomas Dwight. *Athenian Tragedy: A Study in Popular Art*. New Haven: Yale University Press. A solid introduction to Aeschylus and the other tragedians.

Greene, William Chase. *Moira: Fate, Good, and Evil in Greek Thought*. Cambridge, Massachusetts: Harvard University Press. Also, New York: Harper and Row, Inc. (Torchbooks). (paperback, 2.75) An outstanding work, with a section devoted to Aeschylus.

Hadas, Moses. *A History of Greek Literature*. New York: Columbia University Press. (paperback, 1.95) A substantial work, with a good discussion of Aeschylus.

Haigh, Arthur E. *The Attic Theatre*. Oxford: Oxford University Press. Needs revision, but still a tremendous compendium of information.

Harsh, Philip Whaley. *A Handbook of Classical Drama*. Stanford, California: Stanford University Press. An excellent work, with a detailed chapter on Aeschylus and his plays.

Kitto, Humphrey D. F. *Greek Tragedy: A Literary Study*. London: Methuen. Also, New York: Doubleday and Company (Anchor Books). (paperback, 1.45) An excellent discussion of the tragedies as literature, with two chapters devoted to Aeschylus.

Mantzius, Karl. *A History of Theatrical Art in Ancient and Modern Times*, vol. I. New York: Peter Smith. Contains a fine section on the development and technique of the Greek theatre.

Murray, Gilbert. *The Rise of the Greek Epic*. New York: Oxford University Press (Galaxy Books). (paperback, 1.75)

Norwood, Gilbert. *Greek Tragedy*. London: Methuen. Also, New York: Hill and Wang, Inc. (Dramabooks). (paperback, 1.75) A substantial discussion, with a chapter on Aeschylus.

Prentice, William Kelly. *Those Ancient Dramas Called Tragedies*. Princeton, New Jersey: Princeton University Press. A scholarly approach to the plays.

NOTES

NOTES

NOTES

NOTES

MONARCH®
NOTES AND STUDY GUIDES

ARE AVAILABLE AT RETAIL STORES EVERYWHERE

In the event your local bookseller
cannot provide you with other
Monarch titles you want —

ORDER ON THE FORM BELOW:

Complete order form appears
on inside front & back covers
for your convenience.

Simply send retail price, local
sales tax, if any, plus 35¢ per
book to cover mailing and
handling.

TITLE #	AUTHOR & TITLE (exactly as shown on title listing)	PRICE
	PLUS ADDITIONAL 35¢ PER BOOK FOR POSTAGE	
	GRAND TOTAL	$

MONARCH® PRESS, a Simon & Schuster Division of Gulf & Western Corporation
Mail Service Department, 1230 Avenue of the Americas, New York, N.Y. 10020

I enclose $ .... to cover retail price, local sales tax, plus mailing
and handling.

Name _____
(Please print)

Address _____

City _____ State _____ Zip _____

Please send check or money order. We cannot be responsible for cash.